VCs of Queen Victoria's Little Wars 1851 to 1901

Kevin Brazier

BARNTHORN
PUBLISHING

For Leif Hedman, much missed by his family.

ACKNOWLEDGMENTS

I must mention a few people; firstly, my thanks to Barnthorn Publishing, in particular Neil & Ashley, for commissioning me to write this book, and Mark Green, for his continued support and research, also for access to his excellent website and photo archive, which can be found at: www.victoriacrossonline.co.uk.

All grave photos are from the author's collection.

Thanks also go to Martin Clift for his assistance with recolouring one of the cover images.

I must also mention the Victoria Cross Trust for their continued support. They do amazing work caring for the graves of VC recipients that do not come under the CWGC; please visit their website at: www.victoriacrosstrust.org.

CONTENTS

Introduction   1

1   1850 – 1868; Taiping Rebellion, Anglo-Persian War, First   2
    Taranaki War, Third China War, Umbeyla Campaign,
    Second Māori War, Shimonoseki Expedition, Anglo-
    Bhutan War, Canada, Gambia, Andaman Islands
    Expedition, Abyssinian Expedition.

2   1871 – 1885; Lushai Expedition, Third Anglo-Ashanti   61
    War, Perak War, Balochistan Campaign, Ninth Cape
    Frontier War, Second Anglo-Afghan War, Naga Hills
    Expedition, Morosi's Mountain Campaign & Basuto Gun
    War, Anglo-Egyptian War, First Sudan Campaign.

3   1888 – 1895; Karen-Ni Expedition & Chin Field Force,   122
    Anglo-Manipur War, Hunza-Nagar Campaign, Second
    Gambia Campaign, Kachin Hills Expedition, Chitral
    Expedition.

4   1896 – 1901; Matabeleland Rebellion, Mashona   136
    Rebellion, Malakand Frontier War, Mohmand Campaign,
    Tirah Campaign, Second Sudan Campaign, Cretan
    Revolt, Boxer Rebellion, Third Ashanti Expedition.

Appendix – Alphabetical List   176

Bibliography   180

INTRODUCTION

This book tells the story of 114 men who were awarded the Victoria Cross (VC) for action during some of the lesser known wars and conflicts during Queen Victoria's reign.

Although some are lesser known, there are still many very interesting stories to tell. Three of the eight men to have forfeited their awards are included. William Manley, the only man to be awarded the VC and the German Iron Cross, and the two Sartorius brothers, Euston and Reginald, are included, as is Andrew Fitzgibbon, who, at 15 years and three months is the youngest VC recipient. There are also the strange stories of the VCs of Hinckley and O'Hea.

All known burial locations are listed, with photos of many of their graves, and the most up to date known locations of their VCs.

1

1850 - 1868

Taiping Rebellion (1850-64)

In 1850 the popular leader Hung Hsiu-ch'üan raised an army of Taiping rebels in the Guangxi Province. His aim was to overthrow the weak Qing emperor, Xianfeng, and declare a utopian, Christian 'Heavenly Kingdom of Great Peace.' The rebels declared their new republic in 1851.

This regime was paralysing trade, so Major Charles George Gordon (also known as Gordon of Khartoum), started a campaign to reduce and retake the rebel strongholds.

With an estimated 20-30 million dead, it is one of the bloodiest wars ever.

George HINCKLEY
FUNG WHA
9 October 1862

George Hinckley VC

George Hinckley was born on 22 June 1819 in Liverpool; he enlisted into the Royal Navy as a young boy.

On 9 October 1862 Hinckley was 43 years old and serving in the Naval Brigade as an able seaman, when he was part of a force attacking the fortified town of Ningbo. They found the main gate blocked and had to retreat under very heavy fire. He then noticed the assistant master of his ship, HMS *Sphinx*, lying wounded in the open. Hinckley ran to him and carried him 150 yards to the safety of a joss-house (a temple or church). Later, he went back to rescue a wounded army captain and then rejoined the fight.

His VC was gazetted on 6 February 1863 and presented to him by Admiral Sir Houston Stewart at Devonport on 7 July 1863. However, later that year Hinckley lost the decoration while attending a funeral (possibly falling into the grave). He requested, and was granted in November 1863, an official replacement.

Hinckley retired from the Royal Navy with the rank of quartermaster and died at his home on 31 December 1904. He is buried in Ford Park Cemetery; Section P, No. 3/R-16, Ford Park Road, Plymouth, Devon.

His VC was sold at auction in 1925, and again in 1962, when it was bought by the medal dealer Baldwin's, who purchased it at auction from Glendining's. The VC was engraved GEORGE HINCKLEY, ABLE SEAMAN, 9TH OCTR, 1862. Almost immediately after this sale the Royal Naval Barracks in Portsmouth claimed they had the real replacement decoration, which they had held for 40 years. This VC was engraved G. HINCKLEY, OCT. 9TH. 1862. A director of Glendining's stated 'we are satisfied that the decoration we sold was genuine after being examined by Hancocks, who gave it a clean bill of health.' On examining the Royal Naval Barracks VC, Hancocks declared that it was an 'excellent copy.'

To make things even more confusing another VC was taken to Glendining's by an anonymous person, claiming it to be the original Hinckley VC. This VC was engraved with GEO. HINCKLEY, A.B., OCTOBER, 9TH, 1862. Hancocks examined it and declared it to be a copy.

The Glendining's VC was next seen when it came up for sale by Sotheby's in 1988, where it was listed as 'The official replacement Second China War VC engraved as above to, GEORGE HINCKLEY, ABLE SEAMAN, 9TH OCTR, 1862.' It was sold to an anonymous buyer.

Another VC is privately held that was acquired from an unknown source in 1991, the buyer believing it to be the official replacement issued to Hinckley in 1862. The engraving on this decoration is AB GEO HINCKLEY, 9TH, OCT, 1862, which is what would be expected of a Hancocks produced VC. However, the provenance of this VC has not yet been proven. The official replacement VC is still not publicly held.

Anglo-Persian War (1856-57)

In the days when Britain ruled India a major influence on British policy was the threat of Russian incursions into this part of the Empire. It was with the Russian threat in mind that Britain helped to create the state of Afghanistan between India and Persia, as a buffer. The British supported the incorporation of the city of Herat into Afghanistan. So when Persia annexed Herat in October 1856, and diplomatic measures failed, Britain declared war on Persia on 1 November 1856.

John Augustus WOOD
BUSHIRE
9 December 1856

John Augustus Wood VC

John Wood was born on 10 June 1818 in Fort William, Scotland. At 21 he joined the 20th Bombay Native Infantry (later the 120th Rajputana Infantry).

On 9 December 1856 he was 38 years old and a captain when he led the Grenadier Company at the head of the storming party at Bushire and was the first man on the parapet of the fort, where he was immediately attacked by a large number of the enemy. A volley was fired at him and his men at very close range, Wood was hit by seven musket balls, but he at once threw himself upon the enemy, killing their leader. He was closely followed by the men of the company who speedily overcame the garrison.

His wounds, although not life threatening, were very painful and debilitating, which forced him out of service for some time. He sailed to Bombay to recuperate from his wounds, returning to Bushire in February 1857, spending eight months with his regiment. Wood finally left Bushire in September, on the Melbourne, and disembarked at Bombay on 20 October 1857. Fully recovered, he served the British in the Indian Mutiny of 1857-59. His VC was finally gazetted on 3 August 1860 and was probably posted to him as there is no record of it being presented.

Wood left the army with the rank of brevet colonel in February 1870 and died from concussion of the brain on 23 January 1878.

He is buried in St. Mary's Churchyard (under the name Augustus John Wood), Poona, India.

His VC was sold by Sotheby's in 1910 and is believed to be held by the Rajputana Rifles Regimental Museum, in Delhi, India.

John Grant MALCOLMSON
KHOOSH-AB
8 February 1857

John Grant Malcolmson VC

John Malcolmson was born on 9 February 1835 in Muckrach, near Inverness, Scotland, the son of James Malcolmson.

On 8 February 1857 at Khoosh-Ab he was 21 years old and serving as a lieutenant in the 3rd Bombay Light Cavalry, when he saw Lieutenant Arthur Moore's horse fall dead and land on top of Moore, breaking his sword. Moore had charged into a square of 500 Persians, jumping over their bayonets and was now trying to fight off the Persians with his broken sword.

Seeing this, Malcolmson fought his way into the square, and offered his stirrup to carry Moore to safety. Had it not been for Malcolmson's help, Moore would almost certainly have been killed.

Malcolmson's VC was gazetted on 3 August 1860 and was presented to him by Queen Victoria at Windsor Castle on 9 November 1860.

He became a Gentleman at Arms in 1870 and lived in London.

Malcolmson died on 14 August 1902 and is buried in Kensal Green Cemetery; Square 99 – RS, Family Vault, Harrow Road, London.

His VC is held by the National Army Museum, London.

Arthur Thomas MOORE
KHOOSH-AB
8 February 1857

Arthur Thomas Moore VC

Arthur Moore was born on 20 September 1830 in Carlingford, County Louth, Ireland, the son of Edward Francis Moore. He joined the 3rd Bombay Light Cavalry as a second lieutenant in July 1850, was promoted to lieutenant in August 1855 and served as adjutant of his regiment.

On 8 February 1857 at Khoosh-Ab he charged into a square of 500 Persians, jumping over their bayonets. His horse fell dead and landed on top of him, breaking his sword. He tried to fight off the Persians with his broken sword. Had it not been for Lieutenant John Malcolmson's (page 6) help he would almost certainly have been killed.

Moore went on to serve the British in the Indian Mutiny taking part in actions at Rathgar, Barodia, Sangor, Garakota, Calpe, and Gwalior, twice being mentioned in despatches.

His VC was gazetted on 3 August 1860, but it is not known who presented it to him; he was serving in India at the time, and it may have been posted to him.

Moore was married to Annie Prentice. At his retirement in 1891 he was a brevet colonel.

Moore died from heart failure brought on by influenza on 25 April 1913 and is buried in Mount Jerome Cemetery; Section C156, No.

14036, Harold's Cross, Dublin 6, Ireland.

His VC was sold at auction for £150,000 to a private buyer in 2004.

First Taranaki War (1860-61)

As more and more immigrants came to New Zealand's North Island in the 1850s, there was an increased demand for land to accommodate them. This land had to be bought from the Māori by the British Government.

As a lever, the Governor announced a policy whereby any land could be bought from an individual and anyone obstructing this would be committing treason. This policy was put to the test when the chief of the local Te Āti Awa tribe received an offer to sell land in North Taranaki.

Not surprisingly the local Māori living there were opposed to this. Although their chief, Wiremu Kīngi Te Rangitāke, wanted no war, he could not let the sale go through. The locals obstructed attempts to survey the area, refused to move out, and built a number of pās (forts). The war began on 17 March 1860 when the British attacked the pā at Te Kohia.

William ODGERS
OMATA
28 March 1860

Williams Odgers VC

8

William Odgers was born on 14 February 1834 in Falmouth, Cornwall. He joined the Royal Navy in 1852.

His first marriage was to Ann May, with whom he had a son. His second marriage was to Jane Stoddon, a widow; they went on to have a son and a daughter.

Odgers served aboard HMS *Niger*, a steam corvette, during the early part of the Third China War, becoming a leading seaman and captain's coxswain. On 1 March 1860 HMS Niger arrived in New Plymouth as escort for the steamer, Adelaide, which was transporting men of the 65th (2nd Yorkshire, North Riding) Regiment of Foot.

To reinforce the garrison at New Plymouth, 48 men and a 12-pounder gun from HMS *Niger* encamped on a hill.

On 28 March 1860 a force of British regulars, local volunteers, militia and some of the detachment from HMS *Niger* marched five miles south of New Plymouth to rescue outlying settlers at Omata, who were vulnerable to attack from Māori raiding parties. The badly led expedition was in disarray by late afternoon and the regulars turned back in accordance with an order to return by nightfall. The demoralised volunteers and militia remained, exchanging shots with Māori skirmishers.

The sound of the firing from Waireka pā alerted the garrison at New Plymouth and, under command of Captain Peter Cracroft, a small naval brigade was sent out to investigate. As soon as they arrived, they were ordered to retire by Lieutenant Colonel George Freeman Murray, the senior British officer present.

Ignoring the order, Cracroft fired rockets into the fort, before leading his men into the attack. Leading Seaman Odgers was in the forefront and, spurred on by the offer of a £10 reward by Cracroft, was the first man to enter the pā and capture the enemy's largest flag.

The attack by the naval brigade enabled the volunteers and militia to retire. Odgers' flag was later flown from the mast of HMS *Niger*.

Cracroft, who had been wounded earlier in the day, was promoted and Odgers recommended for the VC, which was gazetted on 3 August 1860. Odgers was also offered a warrant rank but declined. This was the first VC to be awarded for action in New Zealand.

After leaving the Royal Navy he served as a coastguard boatman in England from 1863 to 1868 and later became innkeeper of the Union Inn in Saltash.

After suffering from consumption for some time Odgers died on

20 December 1873. He is buried in St. Stephen's Parish Churchyard, Saltash, Cornwall.

His VC was sold in the 1920s and is held by the Sheesh Mahal Museum, Patiala, Punjab, India.

John LUCAS
HUIRANGI BUSH
18 March 1861

John Lucas VC

John Lucas was born in 1826 in Bagenalstown, County Carlow, Ireland. He was a career soldier, having enlisted into the 40th (2nd Somersetshire) Regiment of Foot (later the South Lancashire Regiment) in the early 1850s.

On 18 March 1861 Colour Sergeant Lucas was acting sergeant of a skirmish party to the right of No. 7 Redoubt, and close to the Huirangi bush, facing the left of the position occupied by the Māori.

At about 4pm a very heavy and accurate fire suddenly opened up on his men. Three men were hit, two of them mortally, and assistance was called for to have them moved to safety. Help was arriving when one of them was hit, and at the same time Lieutenant Rees was wounded.

Under heavy fire from only 30 yards Lucas ran to assist Rees and sent a man back with him to the rear. He then took charge of the arms of the killed and wounded, took post behind a tree, and returned fire for 15 minutes until support arrived.

His VC, gazetted 19 July 1861, was presented to him at a full parade at Ellerslie Racecourse, Auckland on 2 October 1861. Lucas was also promoted to sergeant major.

After his army career he returned to Ireland, where he died on 4 March 1892. He is buried in St. James's Churchyard (the church itself now being a distillery), James Street, Dublin, Ireland. His headstone was rumoured to have been damaged during the Easter Rising of 1916 but has since been repaired and placed close to his grave.

His VC is held by the Lancashire Infantry Museum, Fulwood Barracks, Preston, Lancashire.

Third China War (1856-60)

Chinese resentment of European traders and diplomats had already resulted in the First China War 1840-42. An uneasy peace came to an end when the Chinese executed a French missionary, and five Chinese sailors were removed from a British ship and tried for piracy. This led to the Second China War 1846-47, which was concluded with the Treaty of Tientsin. When the British and French commissioners set sail up the Pei Ho (or Hai) River to ratify the treaty they were fired on from the three Taku Forts, thus starting the Third China War.

The two Chinese guns at the Woolwich arsenal, now used to make the Victoria Cross, were most likely captured at the Taku Forts.

Nathaniel Godolphin BURSLEM
TAKU FORTS
21 August 1860

Nathaniel Godolphin Burslem VC

Nathaniel Burslem was born on 2 February 1837 in Limerick, Ireland, the son of George James Burslem (of the 94th Regiment of Foot) and Susan née Vokes. His family can trace their name back to the town of Burslem in Staffordshire. His Grandfather was Colonel Nathaniel Godolphin Burslem, who was awarded the Army Gold Medal.

He joined the 67th (South Hampshire) Regiment of Foot (later the Royal Hampshire Regiment) as an ensign in February 1858 and was posted to China in 1860.

Major General Sir Robert Napier's aim was to force the Chinese from the Taku Forts positioned at the mouth of the Pei Ho River, with an Anglo-French force.

The assault began at 6am on 21 August 1860. The attackers surged forward, crossing a dry ditch and moving through the abatis, then across two wet ditches with great difficulty. Upon reaching the walls the French erected ladders, only to have them thrown down by the Chinese. The men were trapped at the base of the walls while under fire from grenades, cannon, quicklime and 'stinkpots' which gave off clouds of smoke.

Lieutenant Burslem and Private Lane (page 13) endeavoured to enlarge an opening in the wall before anyone else. They forced their way in and were both severely wounded.

After recovering from his wounds Burslem was transferred to the 60th (The King's Royal Rifles Corps), as a captain.

His VC, gazetted 13 August 1861, was presented to him by the General Officer Commanding Canada, Major General Sir William Williams in Montreal in September 1862.

Burslem remained in the army until 1864, when he retired by selling his commission, and emigrating to New Zealand.

Tragically on 14 July 1865, at just 28 years old, Burslem drowned in a boating accident in the Thames River, near Auckland. His body was never recovered.

Burslem's VC is held by the Royal Hampshire Regiment Museum, Winchester, Hampshire.

His third cousin, Robert Shebbeare, was also awarded the VC, during the Indian Mutiny.

Thomas LANE
TAKU FORTS
21 August 1860

Thomas Lane VC

Thomas Lane was born in May 1836 in County Cork, Ireland. He fought in the Crimean War with the 47th Regiment of Foot and served the British in the Indian Mutiny. He then joined the 67th (South Hampshire) Regiment of Foot (later the Royal Hampshire Regiment) just in time to be shipped to China.

Major General Sir Robert Napier's aim was to force the Chinese from the Taku Forts positioned at the mouth of Pei Ho River, with an Anglo-French force.

The assault began at 6am on 21 August 1860. The attackers surged forward, crossing a dry ditch and moving through the abatis, then across two wet ditches with great difficulty. Upon reaching the walls the French erected ladders, only to have them thrown down by the Chinese. The men were trapped at the base of the walls while under fire from grenades, cannon, quicklime and 'stinkpots' which gave off clouds of smoke.

Lieutenant Burslem (page 12) and Private Lane endeavoured to enlarge an opening in the wall before anyone else. They forced their way in and were both severely wounded.

His VC, gazetted 13 August 1861, was presented to him by Brigadier Staveley in Shanghai on 28 November 1862.

Lane left the army and moved to South Africa, joining the police.

He fought in the Anglo-Zulu War as a sergeant in the 3rd Natal Native Contingent, and in the Basuto War of 1881-82.

Lane was a habitual drinker and was convicted of desertion and the theft of 'a horse, arms and accoutrements' in 1881. Due to his conviction he was the subject of a Forfeiture Warrant signed by the Sovereign, meaning his decoration was to be returned. However, he was not struck off the Register of the VC, as only the decoration and pension were forfeited.

This practice was discontinued in 1920 when George V was so concerned by the prospect of future forfeits that it was declared: 'The King feels so strongly that, no matter the crime committed by anyone on whom the VC has been conferred, the decoration should not be forfeited. Even were a VC [recipient] be sentenced to be hanged for murder, he should be allowed to wear his VC on the scaffold.'

Although Lane gave himself up, his VC and other medals had been given to a friend for safekeeping, but the War Office demanded their return by the authorities in South Africa. To avoid the wrath of the War Office, and having some spare VCs available for local issue, a VC complete with Lane's details was returned to London, thinking that would be an end to it.

Lane died from inflammation of the lungs on 12 April 1889, and is buried in Gladstone Cemetery; RC Section, Row 4, Grave 23,

Kimberley, South Africa.

In 1909 two officers of the Hampshire Regiment discovered Lane's original VC and other medals in a pawn shop in Pietermaritzburg and had them sent to regimental headquarters in Winchester.

The 'War Office' VC eventually found its way onto the market, where it changed hands a number of times and much debate ensued as to which was the original.

In 1977, through examination and x-rays, it was proved that the VC held in the regimental headquarters was the original being identical in metal content and engraving to the other three VCs held by them (Burslem (page 12), Lenon (page 18) and Chaplin (page 19)). The 'War Office' VC was examined and found to have the same metal content, but the engraving was inconsistent with the other VCs. This VC was again sold at auction and the purchaser donated it to the Royal Hampshire Regiment Museum, Winchester, where both decorations are now held.

Robert Montresor ROGERS
TAKU FORTS
21 August 1860

Robert Montresor Rogers VC

Robert Rogers was born on 4 September 1834 in Dublin, Ireland. He joined the 44th (East Essex) Regiment of Foot (later the Essex Regiment) in February 1855 and was commissioned a lieutenant in

August of the same year.

He fought with distinction in the Crimean War, where he served during the later part of the siege and fall of Sebastopol. Following the Crimean War he was posted to China.

Major General Sir Robert Napier's aim was to force the Chinese from the Taku Forts positioned at the mouth of Pei Ho River, with an Anglo-French force.

The assault began at 6am on 21 August 1860. The attackers surged forward, crossing a dry ditch and moving through the abatis, then across two wet ditches with great difficulty. Upon reaching the walls the French erected ladders, only to have them thrown down by the Chinese. The men were trapped at the base of the walls while under fire from grenades, cannon, quicklime and 'stinkpots' which gave off clouds of smoke.

During the storming of the Taku Forts, Rogers, with Lieutenant Lenon (page 18) and Private McDougall (page 17), sprang into a ditch in front of the North Taku Fort, swam to the walls and forced their way over the ramparts by using their swords pushed into the walls as a makeshift ladder. Rogers was the first man to gain a footing on the walls and was wounded during the assault.

It would seem likely that the French troops gained entry to the fort first as Rogers', Lenon's and McDougall's citations all say, 'they were the first of the English established on the walls of the fort.'

Following the campaign Rogers was promoted to captain.

His VC, gazetted 13 August 1861, was presented to him by the Commander-in-Chief India, Sir Hugh Rose, on 22 November 1862 in Bengal.

He was promoted to major in 1873 and commanded the 90th Light Infantry throughout the Anglo-Zulu War, being present at Zunguin Nek and Khambula.

Rogers retired with the rank of major general.

He died on 5 February 1895 and is buried in All Saints Churchyard, Church Close, Maidenhead, Berkshire.

His VC is in The Ashcroft Gallery, Imperial War Museum, London.

John Leishman McDOUGALL
TAKU FORTS
21 August 1860

John McDougall was born in 1839 in Edinburgh. He enlisted into the 44th (East Essex) Regiment of Foot (later the Essex Regiment) and was posted to China.

Major General Sir Robert Napier's aim was to force the Chinese from the Taku Forts positioned at the mouth of Pei Ho River, with an Anglo-French force.

The assault began at 6am on 21 August 1860. The attackers surged forward, crossing a dry ditch and moving through the abatis, then across two wet ditches with great difficulty. Upon reaching the walls the French erected ladders, only to have them thrown down by the Chinese. The men were trapped at the base of the walls while under fire from grenades, cannon, quicklime and 'stinkpots' which gave off clouds of smoke.

During the storming of the Taku Forts, McDougall, with Lieutenants Rogers (page 15) and Lenon (page 18), sprang into a ditch in front of the North Taku Fort, swam to the walls and forced their way over the ramparts by using their swords pushed into the walls as a makeshift ladder. McDougall was the second man to gain a footing on the walls.

It would seem likely that the French troops gained entry to the fort first as McDougall's, Lenon's and Rogers' citations all say, 'they were the first of the English established on the walls of the fort.'

McDougall's VC, gazetted 13 August 1861, was presented to him by Brigadier General Frank Adams in Belgaum, India on 2 October 1862. He left the army soon after and returned to Scotland.

McDougall fell ill and died on 10 March 1869, at the age of 30.

He is buried in Old Calton Cemetery, Waterloo Place, Edinburgh.

His VC and China War Medal were stolen from a house in Scotland in 1960, leaving the suspension bars and ribbons behind, which are now on display at the Essex Regiment Museum, Chelmsford, Essex.

Edmund Henry LENON
TAKU FORTS
21 August 1860

Edmund Henry Lenon VC

Lenon was born on 26 August 1838 in Mortlake, Surrey. He enlisted into the 67th (South Hampshire) Regiment of Foot (later the Royal Hampshire Regiment) and was posted to China.

Major General Sir Robert Napier's aim was to force the Chinese from the Taku Forts positioned at the mouth of Pei Ho River, with an Anglo-French force.

The assault began at 6am on 21 August 1860. The attackers surged forward, crossing a dry ditch and moving through the abatis, then across two wet ditches with great difficulty. Upon reaching the walls the French erected ladders, only to have them thrown down by the Chinese. The men were trapped at the base of the walls while under fire from grenades, cannon, quicklime and 'stinkpots' which gave off clouds of smoke.

During the storming of the Taku Forts Lenon, with Lieutenant Rogers (page 15) and Private McDougall (page 17), sprang into a ditch in front of the North Taku Fort, swam to the walls and forced their way in over the ramparts by using their swords pushed into the walls as a makeshift ladder. Lenon was the third man to gain a footing on the walls.

It would seem likely that the French troops gained entry to the fort first as Lenon's, Rogers' and McDougall's citations all say, 'they were the first of the English established on the walls of the fort.'

His VC gazetted 13 August 1861 was presented to him by the General Officer Commanding Ireland, General Sir George Brown at Kilmainham, Ireland on 19 August 1862.

Lenon retired from the army in 1869 and went to the London Stock Exchange, where he made a considerable amount of money. Unfortunately he lost most of it later through speculation. To raise money he pawned his VC and China Medal for 10 shillings.

Lenon died from aortic stenosis and dropsy on 15 April 1893 and was buried in a pauper's grave in Kensal Green Cemetery; Square 154/2, Grave 34010, Harrow Road, London. A headstone was placed on his grave in 2007.

His VC is held by the Royal Hampshire Regiment Museum, Winchester, Hampshire.

John Worthy CHAPLIN
TAKU FORTS
21 August 1860

John Worthy Chaplin VC

John Chaplin was born on 23 July 1840 in Ramsdell, Hampshire, the son of William James Chaplin, Member of Parliament for Salisbury, and Elizabeth (née Alston). He was educated at Harrow and entered the 67th (South Hampshire) Regiment of Foot (later the Royal

Hampshire Regiment) in April 1858.

Major General Sir Robert Napier's aim was to force the Chinese from the Taku Forts positioned at the mouth of Pei Ho River, with an Anglo-French force.

The assault began at 6am on 21 August 1860. The attackers surged forward, crossing a dry ditch and moving through the abatis, then across two wet ditches with great difficulty. Upon reaching the walls the French erected ladders, only to have them thrown down by the Chinese. The men were trapped at the base of the walls while under fire from grenades, cannon, quicklime and 'stinkpots' which gave off clouds of smoke.

Chaplin planted the regimental colour on the breach made by the storming party. He then planted the colour on the bastion of the fort, which he was the first to mount. At this point the Chinese will to resist was broken. Chaplin was severely wounded during this action.

Chaplin's VC was gazetted on 13 August 1861; he was promoted to captain in the 8th Hussars in 1864, and to major in 1878.

From 1868 to 1874 he was an extra aide-de-camp to the Lord Lieutenant of Ireland. He married Isabel Thompson in August 1871.

Chaplin was promoted to lieutenant colonel and commanded the 8th Hussars in Afghanistan 1879-80. Placed on half pay in 1883, Chaplin retired in 1887 to Kibworth House.

Chaplin died on 18 August 1920 and is buried in Kibworth Harcourt Parish Churchyard, Leicestershire.

His VC is held by the Royal Hampshire Regiment Museum, Winchester, Hampshire.

Andrew FITZGIBBON
TAKU FORTS
21 August 1860

Andrew Fitzgibbon was born on 13 May 1845 in Panagarh, Gujarat, India, the son of Quartermaster Sergeant William Fitzgibbon. He joined the Indian Medical Establishment of the Indian Army at the age of 13. In February 1860 he sailed for China attached to the 67th (South Hampshire) Regiment of Foot (later the Royal Hampshire Regiment).

On 21 August 1860 when within 500 yards of the North Taku Fort he proceeded under heavy fire to attend to a wounded dhooli-bearer (stretcher-bearer) and, while the regiment was advancing under the enemy's fire, he ran across open ground to attend to the wounds of Lieutenant Gye. During this act he was severely wounded.

He was gazetted, incorrectly as Arthur Fitzgibbon, for the VC on 13 August 1861, but there is no record of it being presented to him and so it may have been posted to him.

Fitzgibbon returned to India and became an assistant apothecary 2nd Class in January 1867, and 1st Class in 1872. In May 1869 Fitzgibbon married Mary Amelia Coleman and they had two children.

He died from a stroke on 7 March 1883, and is buried in an unmarked grave, Old Delhi Military Cemetery (The Nicholson Cemetery), India. His VC is believed to have been buried with him.

At fifteen years and three months Fitzgibbon is the youngest recipient of the VC. For many years it was believed that Andrew Fitzgibbon and Thomas Flynn were the joint youngest recipients of the VC, however recent research by Shane McCormack and Gearóld O'Brien has shown that Flynn was born on 22 December 1839, making him eighteen at the time of his VC action.

Umbeyla Campaign (1863)

During the late 1850s, the Peshawar district of British-held India came under frequent attack by the Hindustani Pathans based in the nearby Mahaban Mountains. The war-like Pathans were violently opposed to British rule. An expedition in 1858 drove them from their base, but by 1863 they had regrouped around the mountain outpost of Malka, so an expedition was sent to destroy Malka.

George Vincent FOSBERY
UMBEYLA PASS
30 October 1863

George Vincent Fosbery VC

George Fosbery was born on 11 April 1832 in Stert, Wiltshire, one of seven children of the Reverend Thomas Vincent Fosbery. He was educated at Eton from 1846 to 1850. In 1852 Fosbery was commissioned into the Bengal Army. He married Emmeline Georgiana in 1858 and they went on to have ten children, many of whom emigrated to Canada.

On 30 October 1863 at the Umbeyla Pass he was a lieutenant in the 4th Bengal European Regiment, aiming to recapture the Crag Piguet after its garrison had been attacked by the enemy. While the Highlanders and Fusiliers gave covering fire using one of Fosbery's inventions, the exploding bullet, he led a party of men up one path while Lieutenant Pitcher led a party up another. He led his men to the top of the cliff two abreast and was the first man atop the Crag. Afterwards he led his men in pursuit of the fleeing enemy and inflicted many losses on them. Pitcher was also awarded the VC for this action (page 23).

Fosbery was promoted to captain in 1864 and his VC was gazetted on 7 July 1865, it is believed that the decoration was posted to him.

Fosbery was promoted to major in 1868 and to lieutenant colonel in 1874. He retired from the army in 1877.

Later he brought the machine-gun to the attention of the British Government. He also invented the Paradox Gun, a shotgun capable of firing both shot and solid projectiles with accuracy, and the Webley-Fosbery Automatic Revolver, an unusual recoil-operated automatic revolver manufactured from 1901 to 1924.

Fosbery died on 8 May 1907 and is buried in St. Mary's Cemetery (also known as Bathwick Cemetery), accessed via the private road off Horseshoe Walk, Bath, Avon.

His VC is held in The Ashcroft Gallery, Imperial War Museum, London.

Henry William PITCHER
UMBEYLA PASS
30 October & 13 November 1863

Henry William Pitcher VC

Henry Pitcher was born on 20 December 1841 in Kamptee, British India, the son of Vincent Pitcher and Rose Mary le Geyt.

He fought in the Indian Mutiny during 1857 to 1858. Pitcher was appointed to the 1st Punjab Native Infantry in March 1858. He was then seconded to the 3rd Punjab Native Infantry as acting adjutant in 1859 and to the 4th Punjab Native Infantry in 1860.

On 30 October 1863 at the Umbeyla Pass he led a party of men up one path, while Lieutenant George Fosbery (page 22) led a party up another, to recapture the Crag Piguet after its garrison had been attacked by the enemy. He led his men up until he was knocked down and stunned by a large stone thrown from above.

On 13 November he led the first charge during the recapture of the same post, having been taken by the enemy again.

For both actions his VC was gazetted on 19 July 1864, it is believed that the decoration was posted to him.

Pitcher died from heatstroke on 5 July 1875 and is buried in Dera Ismail Khan Cemetery, Kohat, India (now Pakistan).

His VC is held by the Jersey Museum, St. Helier, Channel Islands.

Second Māori War (1863-66)

The truce which ended the First Māori War of 1861 had dealt only with the immediate territorial problems. By 1863 there was an increasing flow of settlers to New Zealand's North Island and the consequent demand for land was again the cause of more fighting.

Edward MCKENNA
CAMERON TOWN
7 September 1863

Edward McKenna VC

Edward McKenna was born on 15 February 1827 in Leeds, Yorkshire. He was working as a wire worker when he enlisted into the 65th (2nd

Yorkshire, North Riding) Regiment of Foot (later the York and Lancaster Regiment) in January 1854. McKenna was promoted to corporal in March 1860, to sergeant in July 1862, and then to colour sergeant in May 1863.

On 7 September 1863 at Cameron Town, New Zealand, when both his officers, Captain Smith and Lieutenant Butler, were shot down, he took command of a small force and charged a much larger enemy force, causing them to disperse into the bush. His force then held its ground under fire and moved on as darkness fell, spending the night in perfect silence, until support arrived at daybreak. For this action he was commissioned an ensign.

McKenna's VC was gazetted on 16 January 1864, and he was presented with it by General Officer Commanding New Zealand, Lieutenant Colonel Sir Duncan Alexander Cameron at Te Awamutu Camp on 18 June 1864.

When his regiment returned to England in 1865, he sold his commission and remained in New Zealand. He joined the New Zealand railways as a clerk and worked his way up to be a station master. Unfortunately his VC was stolen in 1868 but an official replacement was issued to him.

McKenna died on 8 June 1908 and is buried in Terrace End Cemetery; Presbyterian Block II, Plot 65, Palmerston North, New Zealand.

His replacement VC is held by the Auckland Memorial Museum, New Zealand.

John RYAN
CAMERON TOWN
7 September 1863

John Ryan was born in 1839 in Borrisoleigh, County Tipperary, Ireland. He enlisted into the 65th (2nd Yorkshire, North Riding) Regiment of Foot (later the York and Lancaster Regiment) and, after promotion to lance-corporal, was posted to New Zealand.

On 7 September 1863 during the attack on Cameron Town, Captain Swift was mortally wounded and lying in the open. Ryan, supported by Privates Bulford and Talbot, rushed out under fire and Ryan carried the mortally wounded Swift from the field. He stayed with Swift while they were surrounded by the enemy, holding him until he died. Bulford and Talbot were awarded the Distinguished Conduct Medal, where Ryan was awarded the VC.

Ryan drowned on 29 December 1863, trying to rescue a drunken comrade.

He is buried in an unmarked grave in Alexandra Redoubt Commemorative Park Cemetery, near Cameron Town, New Zealand.

Ryan's VC was gazetted on 16 January 1864. His VC was sent to his mother in Ireland who sadly had to sell it in 1902, for £58.

It is now held by the York & Lancaster Regimental Museum, Rotherham, Yorkshire.

John Thornton DOWN
POUTOKO
2 October 1863

John Thornton Down VC

John Down was born on 2 March 1842 in Fulham, London. He enlisted into the 57th (West Middlesex) Regiment of Foot (later the Middlesex Regiment) and was posted to New Zealand as an ensign.

On 2 October 1863 he volunteered to go with Drummer Stagpoole (page 27) to rescue a wounded man lying in the open. They succeeded in bringing back this man who was lying some 50 yards from the bush, which was swarming with Māori, even though the enemy kept up a very heavy fire at short range.

His VC was gazetted on 22 September 1864 and was presented to him later that year by the General Officer Commanding New Zealand, Lieutenant Colonel Sir Duncan Alexander Cameron.

Down died from fever on 27 April 1866 and is buried in Ōtāhuhu Old Cemetery; Block B, Plot 24, South Auckland, New Zealand.

His VC location is not publicly held.

Dudley STAGPOOLE
POUTOKO
2 October 1863

Dudley Stagpoole VC

Dudley Stagpoole was born in 1838 at Killunan, County Galway, Ireland, the youngest of three boys, of whom only he has a recorded date of birth. He enlisted as a drummer into the 57th (West Middlesex) Regiment of Foot (later the Middlesex Regiment), in May 1854. He served in the Crimean War before being posted to New Zealand.

On 25 September 1863 at Kaipakopako, despite being wounded in the head, he twice volunteered to help wounded men who were lying in the open and under fire. For this action he was awarded the Distinguished Conduct Medal.

Then, just a week later on 2 October, he volunteered to go with Ensign Down (page 26) to rescue a wounded man lying in the open. They succeeded in bringing back this man who was lying some 50 yards from the bush, which was swarming with Māori who were keeping up a very heavy fire at short range.

His VC was gazetted on 22 September 1864 and was presented to him at the same time as Down's.

Stagpoole served a total of 21 years; as well as in the Crimea and New Zealand, he saw service in India and Malta. After leaving the army, he married three times and had a total of seven children.

Stagpoole died on 1 August 1911 and is buried in Hendon Cemetery & Crematorium; Section B-8, Grave 15694, Holders Hill Road, London.

His VC is held by the 3rd Battalion, Princess of Wales's Royal Regiment Headquarters, Dover Castle, Canterbury, Kent.

William TEMPLE
RANGIRIRI
20 November 1863

William Temple VC

William Temple was born on 7 November 1833 in Monaghan Town, Ireland, the son of Doctor William Temple and Anne Temple. He was educated privately at the Reverend John Bleckley School and later at Trinity College, Dublin. After qualifying he entered the army in November 1858 as an assistant surgeon on the staff and in January 1859 was appointed assistant surgeon in the Royal Regiment of Artillery.

In November 1860 he was posted to New Zealand, where in October 1862 he married Anne Theodosia, and they went on to have eight children together.

On 20 November 1863 at Rangiriri during the assault on the enemy's pā, he and Lieutenant Pickard (see below) exposed themselves to great danger in crossing the entrance at a point where the enemy were concentrating their fire, in order to assist the wounded Captain Mercer. Temple dressed Mercer's wounds, while Pickard went back and forth to bring water.

His VC was gazetted on 23 September 1864, and from 1868 to 1873 he was surgeon to the Army Medical Department. Temple was promoted to surgeon major in charge of the Station Hospital at Southsea. After a period as staff surgeon he was posted to India from 1884 to 1889, and while there served as lieutenant colonel and secretary to the surgeon general of the Indian Army Medical Services.

In April 1888 he was appointed brigade surgeon and became honorary surgeon to the Viceroy of India. Temple retired as a lieutenant colonel in November 1889 and returned to England.

Temple died after a long illness on 13 February 1919, and is buried in Highland Road Cemetery, Section R, Highland Road, Southsea, Portsmouth, Hampshire.

His VC is held by his family.

Arthur Frederick PICKARD
RANGIRIRI
20 November 1863

Arthur Fredrick Pickard VC

Arthur Pickard was born on 12 April 1844 in Worksop, Nottinghamshire, the third son of Henry William Pickard and his wife Elizabeth. He enlisted into the Royal Regiment of Artillery and was promoted to lieutenant in 1858, before being posted to New Zealand.

On 20 November 1863 at Rangiriri during the assault on the enemy's pā, he and Assistant Surgeon Temple (page 28) exposed themselves to great danger in crossing the entrance to the pā at a point where the enemy were concentrating their fire, in order to assist the wounded Captain Mercer. Temple dressed Mercer's wounds, while Pickard went back and forth to bring water.

His VC was gazetted on 23 September 1864, and he was presented with it by Major General Ridley in Dublin on 13 April 1865.

Pickard was initiated into the Freemason's Friends of Council Lodge No. 1383 in July 1872. He later became a joining member of the Lodge of Friendship in 1875 by which time he had been promoted to major.

He was appointed equerry to Duke of Connaught (who was also a member of the Friendship) in 1871 and later equerry to Queen Victoria. Pickard eventually made colonel and Companion of the Most Honourable Order of the Bath.

Pickard died from tuberculosis on 1 March 1880 and is buried in Cimetière du Grand Jas, 11th Allee, Cannes, France.

His VC is in The Ashcroft Gallery, Imperial War Museum, London.

Charles HEAPHY
MANGAPIKO RIVER
11 February 1864

Charles Heaphy VC

Charles Heaphy was born in 1821 in London, the youngest of five children of Thomas Heaphy and Mary, who died during his early childhood. Thomas remarried but Charles left home shortly after his father died in 1835 and was employed by the London and Birmingham Railway Company as a draughtsman. In 1837 he entered the Royal Academy and attended classes over the next two years.

Heaphy joined the New Zealand Company as a draughtsman in May 1839 and sailed on the Tory, arriving in New Zealand in August. He was subsequently employed as an assistant surveyor.

In April 1840 he accompanied an expedition to the Chatham Islands, where he was wounded during a skirmish. In the hope of finding a 'great plain', Heaphy began a series of journeys into the hinterland in November 1843.

In February 1846 together, with William Fox, Thomas Brunner and Kehu, he ventured via Rotoiti and Rotorua down the Buller River as far as the commencement of the gorge.

Heaphy lived in poverty from January 1845, his only income a few portraits of acquaintances, some contract survey work and paid militia service.

In 1847 he applied for a post with the colonial government and in

August 1848 was appointed as a draughtsman in the survey office there. He married Catherine Letitia Churton in October 1851. They had no children of their own but took in a boy and a girl belonging to her family as wards.

In 1853 he served as secretary to Governor George Grey on a voyage with Bishop George Augustus Selwyn to the New Hebrides and Norfolk Island.

Heaphy continued working as a surveyor and in 1859 he joined the Auckland Rifles Volunteers, being commissioned a lieutenant in August 1863. He was a propagandist in favour of the war in Taranaki and was involved in surveying the military road being driven south from Auckland.

On 11 February 1863 at the Mangapiko Stream, Major Heaphy went to the assistance of a soldier of the 40th Regiment who had fallen wounded into a hollow, where the Māori were concealed in great numbers. A volley was fired at Heaphy from close range and he was hit by three bullets. He stayed with the wounded man, assisting him all day.

His VC was gazetted on 8 February 1867 and presented to him at a parade in Auckland on 11 May 1867.

In June 1867 he was elected unopposed to the New Zealand Parliament, although he worked hard his time in office was undistinguished, serving until 1869. During this time he also invested heavily, but without any return, in a gold mining company. Much of his later life was spent in fieldwork which left him almost crippled with rheumatism. He was appointed a judge in 1878, but only served for two years.

Heaphy died from tuberculosis on 3 August 1881 and is buried in Toowong Cemetery; Portion 1, Section 5, AL/34, 8th Avenue, Grave 252, Brisbane, Australia.

His VC is held by the Auckland War Memorial Museum, New Zealand.

The Heaphy River was named in his honour.

John Carstairs MCNEILL
ŌHAUPŌ
30 March 1864

John Carstairs McNeill VC

John McNeill was born on 29 March 1831 in Colonsay, Scotland, the son of Captain Alexander McNeill and Anne Elizabeth McNeill (née Carstairs). He was educated at St Andrews College and at the Addiscombe Military Seminary.

He joined the 12th Bengal Native Infantry, who mutinied in 1857. During the Indian Mutiny, near Kaiserbagh in March 1858 he was informed by a native that two English women were hiding nearby. In fact they had been held prisoner for five months by the mutineers. In an operation that captured the imagination of the British public, McNeill and another officer rescued Annie Orr and Madelaine Jackson. For this action he was mentioned in despatches.

After the Mutiny he was appointed aide-de-camp to General Sir Edward Lugard and served in the 107th (Bengal Infantry) Regiment of Foot. McNeil was promoted to captain in 1860, to major in 1861 and then to lieutenant colonel in 1864.

On 30 March 1864 Privates Vosper and Gibson were sent to escort Lieutenant Colonel McNeill to Te Awamutu. On the return journey McNeill observed a group of natives to their front. He sent Gibson back to bring up the infantry while he and Vosper proceeded to high ground to observe the enemy. Suddenly, they were ambushed by 50

33

natives. They turned to gallop back but Vosper's horse went down under a hail of bullets. McNeill rode after the horse, caught it and helped Vosper to re-mount. Although the enemy were very close and firing sharply, they managed to get away by hard galloping.

McNeill's VC was gazetted on 16 August 1864 and presented to him by the Governor of New Zealand, Sir George Grey in Auckland on 6 December 1864. He then commanded the Tipperary Flying Column during the Fenian Rising in 1866-67. He was appointed military secretary to Lord Lisgar, Governor General of Canada, a post he held until 1872. Now a colonel he was placed second-in-command for the Ashanti Campaign of 1873, where he was severely wounded and was twice mentioned in despatches. He said of his wound, 'An infernal scoundrel out there has shot me through the arm.'

He was appointed equerry to Queen Victoria and aide-de-camp to HRH the Commander in Chief. McNeill served in the Egyptian Campaign of 1882 and was promoted to major general. His last post before retiring was as equerry to Edward VII.

McNeill died on 25 May 1904 and is buried in the family chapel at Oronsay Priory, Isle of Colonsay, Scotland.

His VC is in The Ashcroft Gallery, Imperial War Museum, London.

William George Nicolas MANLEY
TE-PAPA
29 April 1864

William George Nicolas Manley VC

William Manley was born on 17 December 1831 in Dublin, Ireland, the second son of Reverend William Nicholas Manley and Elizabeth Browne. He was educated at Blackheath Proprietary School and became a member of The Royal College of Surgeons in 1852.

In 1854 he joined the Army Medical Staff and was attached to the Royal Regiment of Artillery serving in the Crimea from June 1855. Manley was present at the siege and fall of Sebastopol. Following the Crimean War he was posted to New Zealand.

On 29 April 1864 at Te-Papa, during the attack on the pā, Assistant-Surgeon Manley accompanied the storming party and attended to the mortally wounded Commander Edward Hay. He then returned to help with the rest of the wounded. He was one of the last to leave the pā.

His VC was gazetted on 23 September 1864.

Manley also served under Sir Trevor Chute at the assault and capture of the Okotukoo, Putahi, Otapawa and Waikohu Palis, was mentioned in despatches and promoted to staff surgeon. In 1865 he was awarded the Royal Humane Society Bronze Medal for saving the life of a soldier who fell overboard from his ship. Manley married Maria Elizabeth Darton in February 1869 at Sheerness, Kent, and they had eight children.

When the Franco-Prussian War broke out in 1870, Manley was placed in charge of B Division of the British Ambulance Corps attached to the 22nd Division of the Prussian Army. He was present at a number of engagements and received the Prussian Steel War Medal and the Bavarian Order of Merit. For his conduct in finding and treating the wounded of the 22nd Division in action at Châteauneuf and Bretoncelles on 18 and 21 November 1870 and the battles of Orléans and Beaugency on 10 December, Wilhelm I, at the request of the Crown Prince awarded Manley the Iron Cross (2nd Class), making him the only recipient of both the VC and Iron Cross.

Manley was also present at the siege of Paris and with the armistice he went into the city with medical supplies for the hospitals. For this care of the wounded he was awarded the French Cross of the Société de Secours aux Blessés Militaires.

He served in the Afghan War of 1878-79 with the Quetta Field Force and was present at the occupation of Kandahar. Manley also saw service in Egypt in 1882, being present at the Battle of Tel-el-Kebir. He was promoted to the rank of deputy surgeon general before retiring from the army in 1884 with the honorary rank of surgeon general.

Manley died on 16 November 1901 and is buried in Cheltenham Cemetery and Crematorium; Section Y, Grave 5336, Bouncers Lane, Gloucestershire.

His VC is held in storage by the Royal Artillery Museum, Larkhill, Wiltshire.

Samuel MITCHELL
TE-PAPA
29 April 1864

Samuel Mitchell VC

Samuel Mitchell was born on 8 September 1841 in Aspley Guise near Woburn, Bedfordshire, the son of a labourer and later minister. Little is known of his early life. Mitchell joined the Royal Navy in 1857 and served aboard HMS *Crocodile* and later at the shore station in Portsmouth, HMS *Excellent*. In 1860 he was posted to HMS *Harrier* and bound for Australia. By 1864 he was a captain of the foretop.

On 29 April 1864, at Te-Papa during the attack on the pā, he came across the mortally wounded Commander Hay, who ordered Mitchell to leave him and look to his own safety, but he refused and carried him out of the pā on his back. Hay died from his wounds the next day.

His VC was gazetted on 26 July 1864 and was presented to him by Governor General of New South Wales, Sir John Young at The Domain, Sydney on 24 September 1864.

Mitchell left the Royal Navy in 1865 and took up gold prospecting in New Zealand. In 1870 he married Agnes, and they had ten children. At some point his VC was stolen, but instead of applying for an official replacement, he had a copy made.

Mitchell drowned in the Hokitika River while trying to rescue a friend on 16 March 1894 and is buried on a hillside near Ross, New Zealand.

His original VC turned up at auction in 1909 and sold for £50. This VC is held by the West Coast Historical Museum, Hokitika, New Zealand. The copy he had made and wore is now on loan to the Victoria Cross Trust based in Doncaster.

Frederick Augustus SMITH
TAURANGA
21 June 1864

Frederick Augustus Smith VC

Frederick Smith was born on 18 November 1826 in Dublin, Ireland. He was commissioned an ensign into the 1st Regiment of Foot (Royal Scots) in January 1849. Smith was promoted to lieutenant in 1852 and to captain in March 1855. He fought at Alma, Inkerman and Sebastopol during the Crimean War.

In 1861 he exchanged into the 43rd (Monmouthshire Light Infantry) Regiment of Foot (later the Oxfordshire and Buckinghamshire Light Infantry) and was posted to New Zealand.

On 21 June 1864, at Tauranga, he was wounded while leading his men in an assault on a Māori position. Ignoring his wounds, he was the first man to jump into the enemy rifle pits and engage them in hand-to-hand fighting, setting a fine example to his men and leading them to victory.

His VC was gazetted on 4 November 1864, and it was sent to him by registered post. He was promoted to brevet major, becoming a major in 1868. Smith commanded the 43rd from 1875-78, when he retired with the rank of lieutenant colonel.

Smith died on 22 July 1887 and is buried in an unmarked grave, Duleek Churchyard; Family Plot. County Meath, Ireland.

His VC is in The Ashcroft Gallery, Imperial War Museum, London.

John MURRAY
TAURANGA
21 June 1864

John Murray VC

John Murray was born in February 1837 in Birr, County Offaly, Ireland. He enlisted into the 68th (Durham) Regiment of Foot (Light Infantry) in February 1852. Promoted to corporal in 1854, he served throughout the Crimean War and was promoted to sergeant in 1860 while stationed in Burma. In 1863 his regiment was posted to New Zealand.

On 21 June 1864 at Tauranga he was wounded while leading his company in an attack on an enemy position. Ignoring his wounds, he ran up to a rifle pit with about ten Māori in it and killed or wounded them all. He then carried on up the works, attacking with the bayonet. During this action he also saved the life of Private John Byrne, who was awarded the VC during the Crimean War.

His VC, gazetted on 4 November 1864, was presented to him by Brigadier General Waddy at Wanganui on 5 December 1864. In 1872 he transferred into the 2nd North Durham Militia for the last year of his service. Murray left the army having served for 21 years.

He died on 8 April 1912 and is buried in an unmarked grave, English Churchyard, near Derrinlough, County Offaly, Ireland.

His VC is held by the Durham Light Infantry Museum, County Durham.

Hugh SHAW
NUKUMARU
24 January 1865

Hugh Shaw VC

Hugh Shaw was born on 4 February 1839 in Madras, India, the son of James Shaw, Inspector General of Hospitals and Ann Shaw (née Hay). He was educated at the Royal Military College, Sandhurst, and was commissioned an ensign into the 18th Regiment of Foot (later the Royal Irish Regiment) in May 1855. Shaw served in the Crimean War, arriving in December 1885 following the fall of Sebastopol in September, remaining until the end of the war.

Promoted to lieutenant, Shaw saw active service in the Indian Mutiny and in 1859 he became adjutant of his regiment, a position he held until he became a company commander in 1864 when his regiment was posted to New Zealand.

On 24 January 1865 at Nukumaru Captain Shaw was ordered to clear the bush of Māori. Having advanced to within 30 yards of the enemy, his men began to take casualties. He ordered his men to take cover behind a palisade (a fence made from strong wooden posts), and then rushed forward with four privates to bring in a wounded man who was lying close to the enemy and brought him back to safety.

His VC was gazetted on 28 November 1865, and he was presented with it while in New Zealand in 1866. In June 1870 he married Emily Sheffield, and they had three daughters.

Shaw was adjutant of the North Tipperary Militia from June 1873 to February 1878, during which time he was promoted to major. In May 1878 he joined the Royal Irish Regiment (the old 18th) and fought in the Second Afghan War of 1878-80.

In 1881 he was promoted to lieutenant colonel and served in the Sudan expedition to the Nile. He was made full colonel in 1885 and given command of a battalion in 1887. Shaw retired later the same year with the rank of major general.

He died on 25 August 1904 and is buried in Highland Road Cemetery; Section N, 33-7, Highland Road, Southsea, Portsmouth, Hampshire.

His VC is held by the National Army Museum, London. I was lucky enough to hold all of the VCs held at the museum, while I worked there.

Shimonoseki Expedition (1863 - 1864)

The expansion of foreign trade into the Far East was causing mounting resentment in Japan and, in 1863, the daimyō of the Chōshū Domain began to expel foreigners from their land around the Straits of Shimonoseki. His ships attacked European and American ships, and naturally they fired back. The British, French, Dutch and Americans formed an international squadron with the intention of wiping out the Chōshū ships and forts.

Duncan Gordon BOYES
SHIMONOSEKI
6 September 1864

Duncan Gordon Boyes VC

Duncan Boyes was born on 5 November 1846 in Cheltenham, Gloucestershire, one of nine children of John and Sabina Boyes. He was educated at Cheltenham College before enlisting into the Royal Navy at 14 years old. Boyes was posted to HMS *Euryalus* and served as part of the East Indies Station.

On 6 September 1864 at Shimonoseki when Midshipman Boyes was 17 years old, during the attack on a stockade, he carried the Queen's Colour ahead of the storming party under a hail of bullets. He and Captain of the Afterguard, Thomas Pride, were only prevented from advancing further by an order from their superior officer. The stockade was taken and destroyed. After the action it was found that the flag had been pierced six times by musket balls.

His VC was gazetted on 21 April 1865, and he was presented with it by the Commander-in-Chief Portsmouth, Admiral Sir Michael Seymour on 22 September 1965 along with Thomas Pride (page 42) and William Seeley (page 43).

Boyes' life took a tragic turn when, on 9 February 1867, he and Midshipman Marcus McCausland were court-martialled for breaking into the Naval Yard in Bermuda. On the night of the incident the two men had been drinking and upon their return had been refused entry as they did not have the required passes. Both men admitted they were guilty and were discharged from the Royal Navy. Boyes took his punishment badly, drinking heavily and suffered fits of depression. He subsequently moved to New Zealand to join two of his brothers at their sheep station. However the scandal seems to have followed him, as he suffered a complete nervous breakdown.

On 26 January 1869 Boyes killed himself by jumping from a window. His death certificate shows 'delirium tremens' (a psychotic condition associated with withdrawal from alcohol) as the cause of death.

Originally buried in the Southern Cemetery, in 1954, he was reburied in Andersons Bay Soldiers Cemetery; Anglican Southern Section, Block 6, Plot 24, Dunedin, New Zealand.

His VC was held by his old school in Cheltenham between 1978 and 1998, and then it was sold at auction to raise money for a scholarship in Boyes' name. It is now in The Ashcroft Gallery, Imperial War Museum, London.

His brother-in-law Thomas Young was awarded the VC for bravery during the Indian Mutiny in 1857, at Lucknow.

Thomas PRIDE
SHIMONOSEKI
6 September 1864

Thomas Pride VC

Thomas Pride was born on 29 March 1835 in Old Bridge, Dorset. Little is known about him until he enlisted into the Royal Navy and by 1864 was a captain of the afterguard on board HMS *Euryalus*.

On 6 September 1864 at Shimonoseki during the attack on the stockade, Pride ran ahead with Midshipman Duncan Boyes, turning and cheering his comrades on, despite being shot in the chest. Pride and Boyes were only prevented from advancing further by an order from their superior officer. The stockade was taken and destroyed.

His VC was gazetted on 21 April 1865, and he was presented with it by the Commander-in-Chief Portsmouth, Admiral Sir Michael Seymour on 22 September 1965, along with Boyes (page 41) and Seeley (see below). When his career in the Royal Navy ended, he was still a captain of the afterguard.

Pride died on 16 July 1893 and is buried in All Saints Churchyard, Branksome Park, Western Road, Bournemouth, Dorset.

His VC is held by the National Maritime Museum, Greenwich, London.

William Henry Harrison SEELEY
SHIMONOSEKI
6 September 1864

William Henry Harrison Seeley VC

Henry Seeley was born on 1 May 1840 in Topsham, Maine, USA. Ordinary Seaman Seeley was 24 years old and serving in the Royal

Navy, when on 6 September 1864 at Shimonoseki he distinguished himself by carrying out a reconnaissance alone to ascertain the enemy's position and then, although wounded in the arm, took part in the final assault on the stockade, which was taken and destroyed.

His VC was gazetted on 21 April 1865, and he was presented with it by the Commander-in-Chief Portsmouth, Admiral Sir Michael Seymour, on 22 September 1965, along with Boyes (page 41) and Pride (page 42).

Seeley died on 1 October 1914 and is buried in Evergreen Cemetery, Stoughton, Massachusetts, USA.

His VC was believed to be in the possession of his granddaughter until 1943, but since then its whereabouts is unknown.

Seeley was the first American citizen to be awarded the VC.

Anglo-Bhutan War (1864-65)

Bhutan lies to the east of Nepal, and in 1864 following a civil war in the region, the victorious leader of the Punakha people had broken with the central administration and set up a rival government. The legitimate governor was deposed so Britain, protecting her interests in her Indian Empire, sent a peace mission to restore order. The British mediated, dealing alternately with the supporters of the deposed and the new government. But the latter rejected all British attempts to broker peace so, in November, Britain declared war on the new regime.

William Spottiswoode TREVOR
DEWANGIRI
30 April 1865

William Spottiswoode Trevor VC

William Trevor was born on 9 October 1831 in Calcutta, India, the son of Captain Robert Trevor of the 3rd Bengal Cavalry and Mary Spottiswoode. When his father was posted to Afghanistan, the whole family accompanied him. In 1842 during the retreat from Kabul during the First Afghan War his father was murdered, and the remainder of the family taken hostage. They were rescued following General Sir George Pollock's reoccupation of the city nine months later.

After their release the family returned to England, where William and his two brothers obtained cadetships at the Addiscombe Military Seminary. On passing out in December 1849 William entered the Bengal Engineers and, after training at Chatham, he was posted to India in 1851. He served in the 'Army of Ava' throughout the Second Anglo-Burmese War under General Godwin and was mentioned in despatches for his actions in the storming of the White House Stockade at Rangoon on 12 April 1852.

Trevor remained in Burma until he was posted to Bengal in 1857. He constructed barracks on a site at Senchal for European soldiers, and would later join the Darjeeling Field Force under Captain Curzon, that was sent to intercept the mutineers from Decca. In 1861 Trevor was appointed Garrison Engineer at Fort William in Calcutta.

However, he did not see the work completed, as in February 1862, he was appointed superintending engineer of the Northern Circle and supervised the completion of the Ganges and Darjeeling Road.

In February 1865 Trevor was attached to the Bhutan Field Force under Major General Tombs VC and, on 30 April 1865, at Dewangiri, Major Trevor led an attack with Lieutenant Dundas (page 47) on a blockhouse defended by 200 men. To gain entry the two men had to climb a 14 foot wall and then enter through a small hole between the wall and the roof. After setting this example the Sikh soldiers followed them in. Both officers were wounded but the blockhouse was taken with 60 prisoners, the rest being killed fighting to the last.

His VC was gazetted on 31 December 1867, and he was presented with it by Major General C. F. Fordyce in Calcutta 23 March 1868. Trevor was promoted to lieutenant general in 1874 and was made special chief engineer for famine relief works, north of the Ganges, and from December 1875 to 1880 he was chief engineer, British Burma. In 1880 he succeeded his brother as director general of railways and in February 1882 was appointed secretary to the Government of India in the Public Works Department, a post he held until his retirement in 1887. Following his retirement he returned to England.

Trevor died on 2 November 1907 and is buried in Kensal Green Cemetery; Square 179/RS, Grave 31775, Harrow Road, London.

His VC is held by the Royal Engineers Museum, Gillingham, Kent.

James DUNDAS
DEWANGIRI
30 April 1865

James Dundas VC

James Dundas was born on 10 September 1842 in Edinburgh, the son of Judge George Dundas (who adopted the title Lord Manor) and Elizabeth (née MacKenzie). He was educated at Edinburgh Academy, Trinity College (Glenalmond) and Addiscombe Military Seminary. On passing out of Addiscombe in June 1860 as a lieutenant, he was appointed to the Bengal Engineers.

He sailed to India in March 1862 and on arrival was posted to the Bengal Sappers and Miners at Rurki. Dundas was appointed to the Public Works Department in Bengal and was soon promoted to executive engineer of one of the most responsible divisions in that presidency. In 1865 he was appointed to the Bhutan Field Force.

On 30 April 1865, at Dewangiri, he led an attack with Lieutenant Trevor on a blockhouse defended by 200 men. To gain entry the two men had to climb a 14 foot wall and then enter through a small hole between the wall and the roof. After setting this example the Sikh soldiers followed them in. Both officers were wounded but the blockhouse was taken with 60 prisoners, the rest being killed, fighting to the last.

His VC was gazetted on 31 December 1867, and he was presented with it alongside William Trevor (page 45) at Calcutta on 23 March

1868 by Major General C. F. Fordyce.

After the campaign was over Dundas rejoined the Public Works Department, returning to England on leave in 1870 and 1877, the second time due to the death of his father. In the summer of 1878, Dundas displayed great courage when, as a passer-by, he rescued an Indian man from a blazing house after part of the roof had fallen in. In doing so, he received severe burns to his hands.

In 1879, Lord Roberts VC selected him to accompany his Field Force as commanding royal engineer on his advance to Kabul. In the autumn Dundas was attached to General Macpherson's Field Force to aid in the destruction of the line of forts held by the enemy. It was while carrying out this work on 23 December 1879, at Seah Sang near Sherpur, that one of the mines exploded prematurely, killing Dundas.

He is buried in Seah Sang Cemetery, near Sherpur.

His VC is in The Ashcroft Gallery, Imperial War Museum, London.

In 2002, the 'Dundas Bridge' built by the Royal Engineers between Kabul and Bagram in Afghanistan, was named in his honour.

Canada (1866)

The Irish American Fenian Brotherhood, determined to free Ireland from British rule, planned to start a war between Britain and the USA. They decided to carry out attacks on the British dominion of Canada. Two raids were carried out across the border in June 1866, and were repulsed by Canadian volunteers.

Timothy O'HEA
DANVILLE
9 June 1866

Timothy O'Hea VC

Timothy O'Hea was born in 1843 in Schull, County Cork, Ireland. Soon after his enlistment into the 1st Battalion the Rifle Brigade (Prince Consort's Own) he was posted to Canada.

On 9 June 1866 a railway car with 800 German immigrants and 2000lb (900 kg) of gunpowder and ammunition stopped at Danville Station. Late in the afternoon O'Hea noticed the ammunition car was on fire. While others took cover, waiting for the inevitable explosion, O'Hea took the keys from the dithering sergeant in charge, rushed to the car, opened the doors, and started throwing burning boxes out of the car. He also made 19 trips to a creek to collect water to suppress the fire. By his actions the lives of all within reach and a good part of the town was saved.

O'Hea's VC was gazetted on 1 January 1867, but it was not until the 26 April that he was presented with it, while still in Canada. The award was not awarded for bravery in action against the enemy, but for bravery in which public property might be saved, under the 10 August 1858 Amendment to the Royal Warrant. Under today's rules he would have been awarded the George Cross.

O'Hea was said to have died in the Tirari-Sturt Desert, Queensland, Australia in 1874 while searching for a lost member of the Leichhardt

Expedition. Graham Fischer was present at the death but does not describe the specifics of the event. However, a book by Elizabeth Reid, *The Singular Journey of O'Hea's Cross*, poses the theory that Timothy O'Hea died in Ireland in 1869-70, shortly after his discharge from the army and has no known grave. His identity and VC annuity were then assumed by his brother John, and it was John who actually died in Australia.

O'Hea's VC was missing for 75 years until it was found in a drawer in an art gallery in Australia. The VC is now held by the Royal Green Jackets Museum, Winchester, Hampshire.

Gambia (1866)

In 1866 British forces were involved in trouble with a West African tribe in the Gambia. An expedition having been organised by Colonel George D'Arcy, with which the tribal land was invaded.

Samuel HODGE
TUBABECELONG
30 June 1866

Samuel Hodge VC

Samuel Hodge was born in 1840 in Tortola, British Virgin Islands. He joined the West India Regiment where he served as a pioneer in the

4th Battalion. He was posted to Gambia with his battalion; black soldiers were being used for garrison duty due to the high number of malaria cases among white soldiers.

On 30 June 1866, at Tubabecelong, Private Hodge was among a party of 17 volunteers to hack their way into the stockade. Both officers and most of the party were killed or wounded, Hodge and Private Boswell being the only two to make it to the stockade, where they began to cut their way in. Boswell was killed after they broke in and Hodge, now wounded, followed Colonel D'Arcy into the town, smashing open two gates with an axe, thus allowing support troops to enter the town. The enemy were routed, and Hodge was proclaimed the bravest man of the regiment.

His VC was gazetted on 4 January 1867, and he was presented with it by Brigadier General Robert Harley at Newton Barracks, British Honduras (now Belize). Hodge died from a fever on 14 January 1868 and is buried in an unmarked grave, Belize City Military Cemetery, Yarborough, Belize.

His VC is not publicly held.

Andaman Islands Expedition (1867)

When Britain needed a new penal settlement to deal with the prisoners from the Indian Mutiny, they returned to the old penal colony of the Andaman Islands in the Bay of Bengal to establish Fort Blair, despite concerns over the native cannibals on the Islands. The Assam Valley put in at the island of Little Andaman, and a small party went ashore, never to be seen again. An expedition was sent to find out what had happened to them. The five VCs of this expedition were not awarded for bravery in action against the enemy, but for bravery at sea in saving life, under the 10 August 1858 Amendment to the Royal Warrant.

Campbell Mellis DOUGLAS
BAY OF BENGAL
7 May 1867

Campbell Mellis Douglas VC

Campbell Douglas was born on 5 August 1840 on Grosse Island, Quebec, Canada, the son of Doctor George Mellis Douglas and Charlotte Saxton Campbell. He was educated at St. John's, Canada and Laval's University, Canada. Following his education he joined the 24th Regiment of Foot (later the South Wales Borderers) as assistant surgeon to the 2nd Battalion. He spent much of his early career in India with his battalion.

On 7 May 1867, at Little Andaman Island, he with Privates David Bell (page 53), James Cooper (page 54), William Griffiths (page 55) and Thomas Murphy (page 57) risked their lives in manning a boat to proceed through dangerous surf to rescue some of their comrades who had been sent to the island to find out the fate of the commander and seven of the crew who had landed from the ship Assam Valley and were feared murdered by the cannibalistic islanders. After one failed attempt due to the boat filling with water, they managed to land and rescue five men.

All five of the rescuers were gazetted for the VC on 17 December 1867 and they were all presented with it by the General Officer Commanding Pegu, Major General Alured Fauncein Rangoon on 16 April 1868.

Shortly after, he married the young widow of Surgeon Valentine Munbee McMaster VC (awarded in 1857, following the first relief of Lucknow, during the Indian Mutiny). He was also awarded the Royal Humane Society Silver Medal.

Douglas retired in 1882 and early the next year he gave the inaugural first aid training course of St. John Ambulance in Quebec, Canada. Douglas was medical officer in charge of the field hospital during the 2nd Riel Expedition of 1885.

Douglas died on 31 December 1909 and is buried in Wells Cemetery; Grave M, Weston-Super-Mare Road, Wells, Somerset.

His VC is held by the Canadian War Museum, Ottawa, Ontario, Canada.

David BELL
BAY OF BENGAL
7 May 1867

David Bell VC

David Bell was born in 1845 in County Down, Ireland. He enlisted with the 2nd Battalion, 24th Regiment of Foot (later the South Wales Borderers) and was posted to India with his battalion.

On 7 May 1867, at Little Andaman Island, he with Assistant Surgeon Campbell Douglas (page 52), and Privates James Cooper (page 54), William Griffiths (page 55) and Thomas Murphy (page 57) risked their lives in manning a boat to proceed through dangerous surf to rescue some of their comrades who had been sent to the island to find out the fate of the commander and seven of the crew, who had landed from the ship Assam Valley and were feared murdered by the cannibalistic islanders. After one failed attempt due to the boat filling with water, they managed to land and rescue five men.

All five men were gazetted for the VC on 17 December 1867, and they were all presented with it by the General Officer Commanding Pegu, Major General Alured Faunce in Rangoon on 16 April 1868. He was promoted to sergeant before retiring to Kent.

Bell died from senile decay on 7 March 1920 and is buried in Woodlands Cemetery: Section CH, Grave 782, Woodlands Road, Gillingham, Kent.

His VC is held by the Lord Ashcroft VC Collection.

James COOPER
BAY OF BENGAL
7 May 1867

James Cooper VC

James Cooper was born in September 1840 in Birmingham. He enlisted into the 2nd Battalion, 24th Regiment of Foot (later the South Wales Borderers) and was posted to India.

On 7 May 1867, at Little Andaman Island, he with Assistant Surgeon Campbell Douglas (page 52), and Privates David Bell (page 53), William Griffiths (page 55) and Thomas Murphy (page 57) risked their lives in manning a boat to proceed through dangerous surf to rescue some of their comrades who had been sent to the island to find out the fate of the commander and seven of the crew, who had landed from the ship Assam Valley and were feared murdered by the cannibalistic islanders. After one failed attempt due to the boat filling with water, they managed to land and rescue five men.

All five of the rescuers were gazetted for the VC on 17 December 1867 and they were all presented with it by the General Officer Commanding Pegu, Major General Alured Faunce in Rangoon on 16 April 1868.

Following his army career and return to Birmingham, his life took a downward turn, and he ended up in extreme poverty.

Cooper died on 9 August 1889 and is buried in a pauper's grave in Warstone Lane Cemetery; Section P, Grave 1428 (which sadly is still only marked with a small wooden cross without his name), Warstone Lane, Hockley, Birmingham.

His VC is in The Ashcroft Gallery, Imperial War Museum, London.

William **GRIFFITHS**
BAY OF BENGAL
7 May 1867

William Griffiths VC

William Griffiths was born in 1841 in County Roscommon, Ireland. Sadly another recipient of whom very little is known prior to his enlisting into the 2nd Battalion, 24th Regiment of Foot (later the South Wales Borderers) and posting to India.

On 7 May 1867, at Little Andaman Island, he with Assistant Surgeon Campbell Douglas (page 52), and Privates David Bell (page 53), James Cooper (page 54), and Thomas Murphy (page 57) risked their lives in manning a boat to proceed through dangerous surf to rescue some of their comrades who had been sent to the island to find out the fate of the commander and seven of the crew, who had landed from the ship Assam Valley and were feared murdered by the cannibalistic islanders. After one failed attempt due to the boat filling with water, they managed to land and rescue five men.

All five of the rescuers were gazetted for the VC on 17 December 1867 and they were all presented with it by the General Officer Commanding Pegu, Major General Alured Faunce in Rangoon on 16 April 1868.

Griffiths remained in the 24th Foot and was killed in action at iSandlwana on 22 January 1879. It is often said that his body was recovered five months later still wearing his VC, but there is no primary evidence to support this. He is buried in an unmarked mass grave on the iSandlwana battlefield, South Africa.

His VC is held by the Regimental Museum of the Royal Welsh, Brecon.

Thomas MURPHY
BAY OF BENGAL
7 May 1867

Thomas Murphy VC

Thomas Murphy was born in 1839 in Dublin, Ireland. He enlisted into the 2nd Battalion, 24th Regiment of Foot (later the South Wales Borderers) and was posted to India.

On 7 May 1867, at Little Andaman Island, he with Assistant Surgeon Campbell Douglas (page 52) and Privates David Bell (page 53), James Cooper (page 54) and William Griffiths (page 55) risked their lives in manning a boat to proceed through dangerous surf to rescue some of their comrades who had been sent to the island to find out the fate of the commander and seven of the crew, who had landed from the ship Assam Valley and were feared murdered by the cannibalistic islanders. After one failed attempt due to the boat filling with water, they managed to land and rescue five men.

All five of the rescuers were gazetted for the VC on 17 December 1867 and they were all presented with it by the General Officer Commanding Pegu, Major General Alured Faunce in Rangoon on 16 April 1868.

After leaving the army he emigrated to the USA, where he died on 23 March 1899. It is believed he donated his body to medical science as he was not buried until December 1902. It is thought that he is buried in an unmarked family grave in Laurel Hill Cemetery; Plot Q,

Grave 361, Philadelphia, Pennsylvania, USA, but this has not been confirmed.

His VC is not publicly held.

Abyssinian Expedition (1867-68)

Theodor, the Christian Emperor of Abyssinia (now Ethiopia), had pursued an anti-Muslim crusade to reform his country. When in 1862 a new British consul arrived bearing a pair of pistols as a gift from Queen Victoria, he suggested that Theodor approach Queen Victoria to negotiate a treaty of friendship, and so a letter was sent. It seems the letter was lost en-route, and on getting no response the volatile Theodor imprisoned the consul (as he had visited the Muslim Sudan) and some British missionaries. Diplomatic means having failed to solve the problem, Britain sent an ultimatum which was ignored. An expedition was sent to attack the mountain capital of Magdala in 1867.

James BERGIN
MAGDALA
13 April 1868

James Bergin VC

James Bergin was born on 29 June 1845 in Killbricken, Ireland. He enlisted into the 10th (North Lincoln) Regiment of Foot in 1862. The following year he transferred at his own request into the 108th Regiment of Foot with whom he sailed to India. In 1867 he transferred into the 33rd (The Duke of Wellington's) Regiment of Foot (later the Duke of Wellington's Regiment [West Riding]).

On 13 April 1868, at Magdala, when the head of his column was held up by obstacles at the gate, Private Bergin and Drummer Michael Magner (page 60) were part of a group of men who climbed a cliff and forced their way in through a strong fence of thorns and fought the enemy hand to hand. Bergin and Magner were the first men into Magdala.

Both men were gazetted for the VC on 28 July 1868, and Bergin was presented with his in April 1869 by Brigadier General James Domville at Belgaum, India. Following his VC action Bergin transferred into the 78th (Highlanders) Regiment of Foot and returned to service in India.

Bergin died from ague and brain fever on 1 December 1880 and is buried in an unmarked grave, St. Patrick's Churchyard (his name is spelt Bergen in the cemetery register), Poona, India.

His VC is held by the Duke of Wellington's Regiment Museum, Halifax, Yorkshire.

Michael 'Barry' MAGNER
MAGDALA
13 April 1868

Michael 'Barry' Magner VC

Magner was born on 21 June 1840 in County Fermanagh, Ireland. He enlisted in the 33rd (The Duke of Wellington's) Regiment of Foot (later the Duke of Wellington's Regiment [West Riding]), before being posted with his regiment to Abyssinia.

On 13 April 1868, at Magdala, when the head of his column was held up by obstacles at the gate, Private Bergin (page 59) and Drummer Michael Magner were part of a group of men who climbed a cliff and forced their way in through a strong fence of thorns and fought the enemy hand-to-hand. Bergin and Magner were the first men through and into Magdala.

Both men were gazetted for the VC on 28 July 1868, and Magner was presented with his on 4 November 1868 by Lieutenant General Sir G. Butler in Portsmouth. Following his retirement with the rank of corporal, Magner emigrated with his family to Australia.

Magner died on 6 February 1897 and is buried in Melbourne General Cemetery; RC Section CC, Grave 300, Victoria, Australia.

His VC is held by the Museum of Victoria, Melbourne, Australia.

2

1871 - 1885

Lushai Expedition (1871 - 1872)

Since 1850, the Lushai tribesmen had gradually migrated from the Chin Hills into Assam, subjugating the local people to their own rule. They remained untouched by foreign influence until Britain annexed Assam in 1862. The Lushai were furious at this foreign intrusion and started raids into British territory, to which Britain responded with punitive expeditions. When in 1872 the Lushai kidnapped a girl, Mary Winchester, a field force was sent out to save her and to punish the kidnappers.

Donald MACINTYRE
LALGNOORA
4 January 1872

Donald Macintyre VC

Donald Macintyre was born on 12 September 1831 in Kincrain, Ross-shire, Scotland. He was educated at Addiscombe Military Seminary and entered the army in June 1850. Macintyre served with the 66th Goorkha Regiment of Native Infantry (later 1st Gurkha Rifles) against the hill tribes of the Peshawar Frontier, including the destruction of the fort and village of Prangbur and the action at Ishkakot during 1852, under Sir Colin Campbell. A year later he was engaged with the expedition against the Boree Afridis.

In 1856, by now a lieutenant, he served under Sir Neville Chamberlain in the expedition to the Kurram Valley in Afghanistan. During 1857-58 he raised what was to become the 4th Gurkha Regiment and on a number of occasions was employed in protecting the hill tribes on the Kale Kumaon Frontier and maintaining order in the area. He was promoted to captain in June 1862 and in 1864 served in the Doaba Field Force in the Peshawar Valley.

On 4 January 1872, while serving in the Bengal Staff Corps and during the assault on Lalgnoora, Macintyre, now a major, was the first man to reach the nine-foot high stockade. Climbing over it he ran into the flames of the burning village, he was followed by his men, who stormed the village.

His VC, gazetted on 27 September 1872, was presented to him during the winter of 1872 after he had been promoted to lieutenant colonel. Macintyre was promoted to full colonel in 1877. His last active service was as commander of the 2nd Gurkhas in the Afghan War. He retired from the Bengal Staff Corps in December 1880 with the rank of major general.

Macintyre died on 15 April 1903 and is buried in Rosemarkie Churchyard; Family Plot, near Fortrose, Scotland.

His VC is held by the Gurkha Museum, Peninsula Barracks, Winchester, Hampshire.

Third Anglo-Ashanti War (1873-74)

In 1872, the coastal fort of Elmina in Ashanti (now Ghana), came into British possession. This was the last outlet for trade to the sea for the native Ashanti people and their King, Kofi Karikari, was ready to fight to protect it. In 1873 he mustered a 12,000 strong army and crossed the Pre River and invaded the coastal area. The British Governor and Commander-in-Chief Major General Sir Garnet Wolseley issued a warning that he was ready to attack, but offered an armistice if the Ashanti would retreat from the coast. Negotiations failed and war became inevitable.

Edric Frederick GIFFORD
BECQUAH
1873-74

Edric Frederick Gifford VC

Edric Gifford was born on 5 July 1849 in Cirencester, Gloucestershire, the eldest son of Robert Francis Gifford (2nd Baron Gifford), and the Honourable Frederica Fitzhardinge. He was educated at Harrow and in 1869 entered the 83rd (County of Dublin) Regiment of Foot.

Gifford was commissioned a lieutenant in the 63rd (West Suffolk) Regiment of Foot in 1872 and later the same year, upon the death of his father, became the 3rd Baron Gifford. In 1873 he transferred into the 2nd Battalion, 24th Regiment of Foot (later the South Wales

Borderers) and was posted to Africa with his regiment.

Throughout the campaign Lieutenant Gifford's conduct was exceptional. He was placed in command of the native scouts and hung upon the rear of the enemy, hindering their movements, noting their positions and capturing many prisoners single handedly. Before the taking of Becquah he entered the city and took note of the enemy positions. He was also at the forefront of the assault on the city.

His VC was gazetted on 28 March 1874, and he was presented with it just two days later at Windsor Great Park by Queen Victoria.

He was promoted to captain in the 57th (West Middlesex) Regiment of Foot in 1876. At the end of the Anglo-Zulu War he was aide-de-camp to Sir Garnet Wolseley and spent two weeks searching for the Zulu King Cetshwayo. He had just found his hiding place when he decided to wait until nightfall to capture the King as his scouts were exhausted. Meanwhile, Major Marter had also found the King's hiding place and marched straight in to capture him.

In 1880 he became a brevet major in the 1st Battalion, the Middlesex Regiment, and in the same year he married Sophia Catherine Street. He was then colonial secretary for Western Australia and a senior member of the Legislative Council from 1880 until 1883. From 1883 to 1888 he was colonial secretary in Gibraltar.

Gifford died on 5 June 1911 and is buried in Burial Ground, Fairfield Road, Bosham, Sussex.

His VC is held by his family.

His nephew John Butler was also awarded the VC in 1914 for action in the Cameroons, West Africa.

Reginald William SARTORIUS
ABOGU
17 January 1874

Reginald William Sartorius VC

Reginald Sartorius was born on 4 May 1841 in Sintra, Portugal, the son of Admiral of the Fleet Sir George Rose Sartorius. He joined the army in January 1858 and in the following May was promoted to lieutenant.

Sartorius fought for the British in the Indian Mutiny, taking part in the Relief of Azimghur, where he volunteered to carry despatches through the encircling enemy, during which his cap was shot through, his head grazed, and he was also shot in the heel. In 1864 he served in the Bhutan War and in 1868 he was promoted to captain.

When, in 1873, a large-scale invasion of the coastal area of the Gold Coast by the Ashanti tribesmen took place, it was deemed necessary to mount a full expedition which was led by Major General Sir Garnet Wolseley.

Major Sartorius was part of a detached column under the command of Captain Glover on the right flank of the main body. Sartorius was later sent out ahead of the column to join up with Wolseley at Kumasi and moved across the entire war zone with 25 men and only 40 rounds of ammunition each.

On 17 January 1874, while serving in the 6th Bengal Cavalry during the attack on Abogu, he went to the assistance of Sergeant Major Braimah, a Houssa non-commissioned officer, who was lying mortally wounded, and brought him to a place of safety while under heavy fire. His VC was gazetted on 26 October 1874, and it was presented to him by Queen Victoria at a Windsor Park Review on 30 March 1875.

Sartorius then joined the staff of the Prince of Wales (later Edward VII) for his visit during 1876-77. He then saw service in the Afghan war of 1878-79. Sartorius was promoted to colonel in 1886, and married Agnes Kemp in 1887. He was promoted to major general in 1895 and retired in 1897, becoming a member of the Royal Yacht Squadron.

Sartorius died on 8 August 1907 and is buried in St. Mary's Churchyard, South Baddesley, Hampshire.

His VC is held by the National Army Museum, London.

His brother Euston Sartorius was also awarded the VC (page 85).

<h2 style="text-align:center">Samuel McGAW
AMOAFUL
21 January 1874</h2>

Samuel McGaw VC

Samuel McGaw was born in 1838 in Kirkmichael, Ayrshire, Scotland, the oldest son of William McGaw and Sarah Thomson. In 1853 the family moved to Kilmarnock for work. In August 1857 McGaw enlisted into the Royal Highland Regiment (later the Black Watch), giving his trade as a mason. His regiment set sail for India the day before his enlistment and he probably joined it there sometime in 1858, taking part in the siege and capture of Lucknow, the assault on Fort Rooyah, the Battle of Bareilly, and the Battle of Sissaya Ghaut.

Over the next few years McGaw was promoted and demoted a number of times. This, however, did not stop him from re-enlisting, when his term of service was about to expire, as a private in February 1867 while in Peshawar. In February 1868 he returned to Scotland with his regiment having served for nine years in India. On arrival he was promoted to corporal but was reduced to the ranks only three months later.

By the end of 1868 the regiment was posted to Aldershot. While on leave in Kilmarnock during 1870 McGaw married a widow, Mrs Ann Stalker. He was promoted to corporal in 1872 and lance sergeant in the following year. In December 1873 he sailed with his regiment to take part in the Ashanti War, arriving just before Christmas.

On 21 January 1873, at Amoaful, Lance Sergeant McGaw, despite having been seriously wounded earlier that morning, led his section through heavy bush, engaging the enemy several times during the day.

His VC was gazetted on 31 March 1874, and he was presented with it by Queen Victoria at Osborne House on 20 April 1874.

In November he was posted with his regiment to Malta, and then in 1878 to Cyprus. Landing on 22 July 1878, unfortunately McGaw died from heat stroke on the march to the camp and is buried close by. Later his remains were moved to the Old British Cemetery, Kyrenia, Cyprus.

His VC is in The Ashcroft Gallery, Imperial War Museum, London.

Mark Sever BELL
ORDASHU
4 February 1874

Mark Sever Bell VC

Mark Bell was born on 15 May 1843 in Sydney, Australia, the second son of Hutchinson Bell. He was educated privately and at King's College, London. Bell entered the Corps of Royal Engineers in 1862 and served in the Bhutan Field Force, 1865-66, commanding the Royal Engineers and the Bengal Sappers and Miners. Next he served in the Hazara Expedition of 1868, being mentioned in despatches for his 600 mile forced march.

On 4 February 1874, at the Battle of Ordashu, Lieutenant Bell was observed to be always out in front, urging on an unarmed working party of Fanti labourers who were exposed not only to enemy fire, but to the wild and irregular fire of the native troops to their rear. He encouraged them to work under fire without a covering party and he contributed considerably to the success of the day.

His VC was gazetted on 20 November 1874, and he was presented with it six days later by Queen Victoria at Windsor Castle.

In 1875 he married Angelina Helen, but sadly she died four years later. Bell was promoted to major in 1882 and brevet lieutenant colonel in 1883. Bell was an intelligence officer during the Burma Campaign of 1886-87, during which time he was promoted to brevet colonel.

Appointed aide-de-camp to Queen Victoria in 1887, he remarried in 1890 to Nora Margaret. Despite being put on half pay due to ill-health, he was well known for traversing over 12,000 miles through uncharted parts of Asia, China and the Far East.

Bell died on 26 June 1906 and is buried in All Souls Churchyard, All Soul's Road, South Ascot, Berkshire.

His VC is held by the Royal Engineers Museum, Gillingham, Kent.

Perak War (1875-76)

Britain, who had occupied Singapore since 1819, had exercised a policy of not getting involved in local upheavals in the Malay states to the north. However, when civil war broke out in nearby Selangor in 1871, Britain intervened, annexing the region. The next year trouble flared up in Perak and threatened to spread to Singapore, so it too was annexed. These areas proved difficult to control, with the British Resident James Birch's measures to keep law and order bringing him into direct conflict with the local Malay leaders.

In July 1875, seeing their power and revenue seriously threatened, the Malay chiefs had Birch murdered. Britain replied with a punitive expedition to find the assassins.

George Nicolas CHANNER
PERAK
20 December 1875

George Nicolas Channer VC

George Channer was born on 7 January 1843 in Allahabad, India, the son of Colonel George Girdwood Channer and his wife Susan Kendall. He was educated in England at Truro and Cheltenham College. Channer entered the Bengal Infantry with the rank of ensign and was promoted to lieutenant in 1861. He served with the 89th and 95th Regiments until 1866. Channer took part in the Umbeyla Expedition on the North-West Frontier of India in 1863-64 and the Lushai Expedition in 1870-71.

On 20 December 1875 he, by now a captain in the Bengal Staff Corps, Indian Army and 1st Gurkha Rifles, was tasked with gathering intelligence on the enemy's strength. He crept up so close to the stockade that he could hear them talking and, seeing there was no watch, he signalled his men to attack. He shot the first man dead himself and was the first man to enter the stockade, which was taken before the enemy could react effectively. His action undoubtedly saved a great many lives, as it would have been necessary to resort to the bayonet.

His VC was gazetted on 12 April 1876 and presented to him later that year.

Channer served in the Jowaki Afridi Expedition of 1877-78.

During the Second Afghan War he was present at the capture of Peiwar Kotal in 1878. In 1878 he married Annie Isabella, and they had six sons, two of whom died young, and four daughters. Channer commanded the 1st Brigade during the Black Mountain Expedition in 1888 and, in the Chitral Campaign of 1895, he commanded the reserve brigade having by then been promoted to major general.

Channer died on 13 December 1905 and is buried in East-the-Water Cemetery; Section C, Grave 505, Bideford, Devon.

His VC was sold at auction in 2016 for a hammer price of £200,000 and is now in The Ashcroft Gallery, Imperial War Museum, London.

Balochistan Campaign (1877)

Two treaties were signed in 1859 and 1876, strengthening Balochistan's ties with the British Indian Empire, and in 1876 British forces set up a strongly garrisoned army station at Quetta in the west of Balochistan, commanding the Bolan and Khojak passes through the mountains.

Andrew SCOTT
QUETTA
26 July 1877

Andrew Scott was born on 22 August 1840 in Devon. He joined the army at the age of 20, becoming part of the Bengal Staff Corps. Scott was promoted to lieutenant in 1862 and then to captain in 1872.

On 26 July 1877, at Quetta, Captain Scott was on duty on the regimental parade ground, when he heard that some British officers were under deadly attack by coolies. He immediately went to their assistance. He found Lieutenant Hewson cut down and the wounded Lieutenant Kunhardt being hard pressed, and only being protected by Sepoy Ruchpul Singh. Scott bayoneted two of the enemy and closed with a third, who fell to the ground and was killed by a sepoy (probably Ruchpul Singh).

His VC was gazetted on 18 January 1878, and he was presented with it in India on 15 April the same year.

He was later promoted to major in the 4th Sikh Infantry and served in the Afghan War of 1878-79.

Scott was killed in action at Srinagar, Kashmir on 5 September 1882 and is buried in Kashmir Cemetery, India.

His VC is not publicly held.

Ninth Cape Frontier War (1877-78)

In 1877 the Ngika and Gaika sections of the Xhosa tribe took arms against the Fingoes, who they felt to be favoured by the British colonists. What started as a beer brawl between two tribes near the old mission station at Butterworth suddenly escalated into full blown tribal conflict.

The ensuing war drew in British forces in support of the colonial police to support the Fingoes against the Gaikas. It was a war of intermittent raids, ambushes, skirmishes and some small, pitched battles around the Cape region, notable for the British using the Gatling gun for the first time.

Hans Garrett MOORE
KOMGHA
29 December 1877

Hans Garrett Moore VC

Hans Moore was born on 31 March 1834 in Richmond Barracks, Dublin, Ireland, the son of Garrett Moore and Charlotte (née Butler).

One of his ancestors was Prince Rory O'Moore who fought with Henry VIII. He was educated at the Banagher Royal School and at Trinity College, Dublin.

He was commissioned (without purchase, due to his family's war service) into the 59th (2nd Nottinghamshire) Regiment of Foot as an ensign in June 1855, but was transferred into his father's regiment, the 88th Regiment of Foot (Connaught Rangers) the following month. Moore was promoted to lieutenant in October 1855 and served with his regiment during the Indian Mutiny, where he was twice slightly wounded, and mentioned in despatches.

He became adjutant of his regiment in August 1863 and held the post until June 1872 when he was promoted to captain. Moore volunteered for the Ashanti War of 1873-74 and, for his service there, was promoted to brevet major.

On 29 December 1877, near Komgha, Major Moore was part of a small force retreating before a large body of Gaikas. Seeing a private unable to mount his horse and with the enemy surrounding him, Moore, realising the danger, turned back and rode into the middle of the enemy to help him. He killed two Gaikas and was wounded by an assegai in the arm, but he was unable to save the private. When the doctor tried to treat his wound by cutting his jacket Moore said, 'Hold on, this is my only coat, rip it up the seam.'

His VC was gazetted on 27 June 1879, and he was presented with it by the Governor of Gibraltar, Lord Napier, on 6 September 1979. Moore, now serving in the Argyll and Sutherland Highlanders, was promoted to colonel in April 1882. He served under his old commanding officer, Sir Garnet Wolseley, during the Egyptian Campaign of 1882. Moore was present at the second action at Kassassin and Tel-el-Kebir, for which he was mentioned in despatches.

Shortly after this campaign Colonel Moore retired from active service and returned to Ireland. He took up yachting but sadly this would lead to his death. On the night of 6/7 October 1889, after dining with General Cooper, Moore rowed out to his yacht, *Foam*, to secure a line to a buoy. He could not row back against the wind and his body was found the following morning.

Moore is buried in Mount Jerome Cemetery; Grave C 25/26-7903. Harold's Cross, Dublin 6, Ireland.

His VC is held by the Museum Africa, Johannesburg, South Africa.

Second Anglo-Afghan War (1878-80)

Britain had been keeping an eye on this important buffer to the north-west of India as part of a 'masterly inactivity' policy. In 1866 the Emir Sher Ali came to power. He was well disposed to Britain and feared Russian intrusion as much as the British. In 1872 Britain and Russia signed an agreement stating that Russia would respect Afghanistan's northern border, and that there would be no need for the British Government to give any promises of support to Afghanistan. Alarm bells sounded when, in 1876, the Emir reluctantly allowed a Russian mission to Kabul, and then refused to admit the British envoy. This intrusion was too close to British ruled India to go unopposed. Sher Ali had to go, an ultimatum was sent demanding a British envoy be admitted and when this was ignored, three columns of British soldiers moved in.

John COOK
PEIWAR KOTAL
2 December 1878

John Cook VC

John Cook was born on 28 August 1843 in Edinburgh, the second son of Alexander Shank Cook, a respected Sheriff. He was educated at Edinburgh Academy and at age 11 was nominated to attend the Addiscombe Military Seminary.

At the age of 17 he was posted to India and joined the 3rd Sikh Regiment as an ensign and served with them during the Umbeyla Expedition, on the North-West Frontier. He was mentioned in despatches for his gallantry in leading a bayonet charge. He also took part in the Hazara Expedition of 1868 and, after ten years' service, decided to take a year off and return home.

Cook returned to India in 1871, was promoted to captain in 1872 and transferred to the 5th Gurkha Rifles. When the Afghan War broke out the 5th Gurkhas joined the Kurram Field Force under Lord Roberts VC.

On 2 December 1878 at Peiwar Kotal, Cook led a charge out of the trenches with such intensity that the enemy broke and fled. During the fight Cook went to the assistance of Major Galbraith who was about to be killed by an Afghan. He parried the man's bayonet and they wrestled for some time until the Afghan bit into his sword arm. Cook hurled him over to give the final blow with his bayonet, but at this point the Afghan was shot in the head. His VC, gazetted on 18 March 1879, was presented to him by Lord Roberts VC in Kabul on 24 May 1879. He would wear it for only seven months.

Promoted to major in November 1879 (but gazetted on 16 January 1880), Cook next saw action on 11 December at Argundeh, where the British were forced back by a large force of the enemy. Cook and his brother, Walter, distinguished themselves by covering the retreat and saving the baggage. Walter received a chest wound and John a head wound.

Major Cook was still able to get about and the next day took part in the attack on the That-i-Shah peak. During this action Cook was wounded in the left leg.

Unfortunately Cook's wound became infected with gangrene, and he died on 19 December 1879. He is buried in Sherpur Cantonment Cemetery, C of E Section, Kabul, Afghanistan.

His VC is in The Ashcroft Gallery, Imperial War Museum, London.

Reginald Clare HART
BAZAR VALLEY
31 January 1879

Reginald Clare Hart VC

Reginald Hart was born on 11 June 1848 in Scariff (or Scarriff), County Clare, Ireland, the eighth child of Lieutenant General Henry George Hart and Frances Alicia. He was educated at Marlborough and Cheltenham Colleges and represented his college at Rugby Union from 1864 to 1865. Hart entered the Royal Military Academy in June 1866 and passed out as a lieutenant in the Royal Engineers in January 1869.

In July 1869 Hart saved a Frenchman from drowning in the harbour at Boulogne-sur-Mer. Hart jumped in from the pier and received a number of injuries but was able to rescue the man. For this he was awarded the Royal Humane Society Silver Medal, a medallion from the mayor in the name of the city of Boulogne and the French Medal of Honour First Class, presented by the President of the French Republic.

In 1872 he married Charlotte Augusta; daughter of Mark Seton Synnot and they had three sons and one daughter.

In October 1872 he sailed to India and on his arrival was posted to the Bengal Sappers and Miners. From September 1874 to March 1878, he was assistant garrison instructor at Umballa. Hart returned to England briefly in 1878 on sick leave but was back in December serving with the Khyber Field Force in the Afghan War. Following this he joined the Second Bazar Valley Expedition against the Zaka Khel

Afridis.

On 31 January 1879, in the Bazar Valley, Lieutenant Hart ran 1,200 yards to the assistance of a wounded sowar who was in a riverbed and exposed to enemy fire. He reached the man as the enemy were about to cut him to pieces, drove them off and brought him back to safety with the help of others.

Hart's VC was gazetted on 10 June 1879, and he was presented with it by Queen Victoria at Windsor Castle on 9 December 1879.

After his investiture he served in the 1st Division of the Khyber Field Force, being employed in reconnaissance. In February 1881, Hart was posted to the West Coast of Africa with Sir Samuel Rowe to the Ashanti War. In 1882 he was promoted to brevet major and served in the Egyptian War, being twice mentioned in despatches, and ending the war as brevet lieutenant colonel.

In 1884 Hart returned to India and in December of that year was awarded a Silver Clasp (Bar) from the Royal Humane Society for saving the life of a gunner who had fallen into the Ganges from a pontoon bridge.

In the Tirah Campaign of 1897-98 he commanded the 1st Brigade and was twice mentioned in despatches. In 1899 he was given command of the Quetta District with a temporary rank of major general. Hart then served on the North-West Frontier before returning to England. He commanded the Cape Colony from 1907-09 and was Commander-in-Chief South Africa from 1912-14. During the First World War Hart was appointed as Lieutenant Governor of Guernsey. After his retirement Hart returned to England.

Hart died on 10 October 1931 and is buried in St. Mary's Churchyard Cemetery, Netherbury, Dorset.

His VC is in The Ashcroft Gallery, Imperial War Museum, London.

Edward Pemberton LEACH
MAIDANAH
17 March 1879

Edward Leach was born on 2 April 1847 in County Londonderry, Ireland, the second son of Lieutenant Colonel Sir George Archibald Leach and Emily Leigh, daughter of Edward Leigh Pemberton. Leach was educated at Highgate School, and at the Royal Military Academy, Woolwich. He passed out in October 1866 and sailed for India in 1869.

From March 1869 to February 1870, he commanded a detachment of the Bengal Sappers and Miners at Rawalpindi, and subsequently joined the Public Works Department in Central India. In October 1871 he was appointed to the Indian Survey and served in his capacity with the Cachar Column of the Lushai Expeditionary Force. In November 1877 Leach went on home leave but was back the following year as private secretary to Sir James Caird, Famine Commissioner. On the outbreak of the Afghan war in 1878, Leach joined the Khyber Survey Party.

On 17 March 1879, near Maidanah, Captain Leach was on a survey reconnaissance with detachments of the Guides Cavalry and the 45th Sikh Infantry, when his party was attacked by tribesmen. While covering the retreat of the survey escort, who were carrying the mortally wounded Lieutenant Barclay, and as the enemy began to press from all sides, Leach led a charge of the 45th Sikh Infantry, killing three Afghans single-handedly and receiving a severe wound to his arm. His actions prevented the annihilation of the whole party.

Leach was back in England due to his wounded arm when his VC was gazetted on 9 December 1879 and was presented with it three days later by Queen Victoria at Windsor Castle. After his wound had healed he was back in Afghanistan in March 1880 and joined the Kandahar Field Force under Major General Primrose, for survey work. He was later appointed brigade major, Royal Engineers, and was present at the final defeat of the enemy by Sir Frederick Roberts VC. Leach was mentioned in despatches four times and ended the war as a brevet lieutenant colonel.

Leach married Elizabeth Mary Bazley in 1883 and they had a son and two daughters. In 1885 he was part of the Suakin Expedition under Major General Sir Gerald Graham VC and was twice mentioned in despatches. After a short spell in England Leach was given command of the 9th Division, 3rd Army Corps in Belfast, before becoming Commander-in-Chief in Scotland, a post he held for four years. In 1905 he was promoted to lieutenant general and in 1910 to general. Leach retired to Italy in 1912.

He died on 27 April 1913 and is buried in Grienze Churchyard, near Cadenabbia, Italy.

His VC is held by the Royal Engineers Museum, Gillingham, Kent.

Walter Richard Pollock HAMILTON
FUTTEHABAD
2 April 1879

Walter Richard Pollock Hamilton VC

Walter Hamilton was born on 18 August 1856 in Inistioge, County Kilkenny, Ireland, the fourth son of Alexander Hamilton, justice of the peace, and Emma Pollock. He was educated at Eagle House, Wimbledon, and Felsted School, Essex. In January 1874 he was commissioned as a second lieutenant into the 70th Regiment of Foot and embarked for India in October 1874.

On being promoted to lieutenant he was offered a commission in the Bengal Staff Corps (Corps of Guides) and within three months had passed the higher standard of examination in languages and was detailed to the cavalry. Hamilton served throughout the Itwaki-Afridi Expedition of 1877-78. He then served as aide-de-camp to the Commanding Officer, General Keyes.

In March 1879 he was present at the operations against the Ranizai village of Skhakat. In October 1879, the Corps of Guides were moved to Jamrud at the mouth of the Khyber Pass and for six weeks were engaged in reconnoitring the mountains. In the first two weeks of the campaign Hamilton participated throughout with the cavalry and was present at the capture of Ali Musjid. In March he commanded a troop on escort duty with a surveying party, during which Captain Leach would earn himself the VC (page 77). At the end of March Hamilton was involved in the advance of General Gough's Brigade toward Futtehabad.

On 2 April 1879, Lieutenant Hamilton led a charge of the Corps of Guides against superior numbers of the enemy. When his commanding officer Major Wigram Battye was killed, Hamilton, the only officer left with the regiment, assumed command and cheered the men on to avenge Battye's death. In this charge, seeing that Sowar Dowlut Ram was down, entangled with his horse and being attacked by three of the enemy, Hamilton rushed over to him and killed all three of his attackers, thus saving the sowar's life.

Shortly afterwards Hamilton was selected to be part of the seventy-man escort for Sir Louis Cavagnari to Kabul. He was killed in action on 3 September 1879 leading a charge against a gun when the British Residency was attacked by the enemy. He is buried in an unmarked grave, in a garden near the British Residency, Kabul, Afghanistan.

Hamilton was recommended for the VC for the action on 2 April 1879, but it was turned down because of his subsequent death.

When Lord Cranbrook was reviewing Hamilton's case he noted that the action was similar to that of John Cook (page 74) and Reginald Hart (page 76), both of whom had been awarded the VC. The VC recommendation was sent in again on 28 September 1879 but, in order to avoid the precedent of appearing to award a posthumous VC, the submission was backdated to 1 September 1879. The award was gazetted on 7 October 1879.

The VC was passed down through the family and is now in The Ashcroft Gallery, Imperial War Museum, London.

Garrett O'Moore CREAGH
KAM DAKKA
21 April 1879

Garrett O'Moore Creagh VC

O'Moore (as he would be known) Creagh was born on 2 April 1848 in Cahirbane County Clare, Ireland, the son of Captain James Creagh RN and Grace Emily O'Moore. He was educated at a private school and at the Royal Military College, Sandhurst. Creagh entered the 95th Regiment of Foot in October 1866, with a purchase as ensign and was posted to India in 1869.

In June 1870 Creagh was promoted to lieutenant and joined the Bombay Staff Corps. He served for a brief time with Marine Battalion and the 25th Bombay Light Infantry and was then appointed officiating-adjutant to the Deoli Irregular Force and station staff officer at Deoli. In 1871 Creagh was selected as adjutant to the Merwara Battalion on its transfer from the civil to military establishment. He married Mary Letitia Longfield, but she died two years later.

In 1878 Creagh was promoted to captain and, when the Merwara Battalion volunteered for service on the outbreak of the Afghan war he was the only European officer present.

Creagh was second-in-command during the campaign in the Peshawar Valley Field Force, until March 1879.

On 21 April 1879, at Kam Dakka, Captain Creagh was ordered to take a detachment of 150 men to protect the village against a threatened incursion of the Mohmands. He had to repel an attack by approximately 1,500 men and the inhabitants of the village who had joined with the Mohmands. His force was compelled to retire, so he took up a position in the local cemetery and held it, repulsing repeated attacks with the bayonet, until the 10th Bengal Lancers arrived, charged the enemy, and routed them.

Creagh's VC was gazetted on 17 November 1879, but there is no record of an investiture. Following his award, Creagh was appointed deputy assistant quartermaster general to the Khurram Field Force and served with them until November 1880. He then served in the Zaimusht and Cham Kanni Expeditions. On his promotion to brigade-major he returned to the Merwara Battalion. From 1882 to 1886 Creagh was in command of the 44th Merwara Infantry, at which time he was given command of the 2nd Baluchis.

Creagh married Lilah Read in 1891 and they had a son and a daughter. In 1895 he was appointed adjutant-general of his division and, in 1896, assistant quartermaster, Bombay Command. From 1898 to 1900 Creagh was political resident commanding in Aden. From 1900 to 1903 he commanded the China Field Force, after which he was given command of the 129th Baluchis. In 1907 he was made secretary to the Military Department at the Indian Office. Promoted to general in 1907 Creagh was Commander-in-Chief India until 1914, and then aide-de-camp to King Edward VII. Following his retirement Creagh was editing *The Victoria Cross 1856-1920*, although sadly he did not live to see it completed.

Creagh died on 9 August 1923 and is buried in East Sheen Cemetery; Section B, Grave 193, Kings Ride Gardens, East Sheen, Surrey.

His VC is held by the National Army Museum, London.

George Stuart WHITE
CHARASIAH & KANDAHAR
6 October 1879 & 1 September 1880

George Stuart White VC

George White was born on 6 July 1835 in Rock Castle, Portstewart, County Antrim, Ireland, the son of James Robert White and Frances Stuart. He was educated at Bromsgrove School, Worcestershire, and at King William's College, Isle of Man. White entered the Royal Military College, Sandhurst, in 1850 and was commissioned into the 27th (Inniskilling) Regiment of Foot in 1853 with whom he served in the Indian Mutiny.

He was promoted to captain in 1863 and transferred into the 92nd Regiment of Foot later (the Gordon Highlanders). White was promoted to major in 1873 and the following year he married Amelia Baly, they had one son and four daughters.

In October 1879 his regiment took part in the advance on Kabul and White, still a major, commanded the right flank. On 6 October, at Charasiah, the artillery had failed to dislodge the enemy from a fortified hill. White led two companies on the position where the enemy outnumbered him by eight to one. When his men became exhausted and immediate action was needed, White took a rifle, ran forward alone, then shot the enemy leader. This decided the issue and the enemy fled.

On 1 September 1880, at Kandahar, White led the final charge at

Kandahar under heavy fire and personally captured one of the two guns held by the enemy, immediately after which they retired.

His VC was gazetted on 3 June 1881, and he was presented with it by the Viceroy of Ripon at Simla, India on 4 October 1881. This was a busy year as White took command of his regiment, was promoted to brevet lieutenant colonel and became military secretary to the Viceroy of India. In 1884 he took part in the Nile Expedition, was acting quartermaster general during the Khartoum Relief Expedition and was promoted to colonel in 1885.

White took part in the Third Burmese War 1885-86 being promoted to major general for his service. He then commanded the Zhob Expedition, and subsequently became Commander-in-Chief in India 1893-98, during which time he was promoted to lieutenant general (1895) and made quartermaster general to the forces (1898-99).

Just before the Boer War White had an accident, leaving him with an injury to his leg. Lord Wolseley told him that he was afraid his lameness must keep him from the front. White's reply was, 'I beg your pardon, sir my leg is well enough for anything except running away.' During the Second Boer War White commanded the Garrison of Ladysmith and held out for 119 days against terrible odds, heavier guns, and the privations and disease caused by a severe siege, afterwards proclaiming, 'Thank God we kept the flag flying.'

In 1900 he was appointed Governor of Gibraltar, and in 1903 was promoted to field marshal. White was governor of the Royal Hospital Chelsea from 1905 until his death there on 24 June 1912.

He is buried in Broughshane Presbyterian Churchyard; Family Plot, Broughshane, County Antrim, Ireland.

His VC is held by the Gordon Highlanders Museum, Aberdeen.

Euston Henry SARTORIUS
SHAHJUI
24 October 1879

Euston Henry Sartorius VC

Euston Sartorius was born on 6 June 1844 in Sintra, Portugal, one of six children (three boys and three girls) born to Admiral of the Fleet Sir George Rose Sartorius. All three boys joined the army. Euston was educated at Woolwich and at the Royal Military College, Sandhurst, after which he joined the 59th Regiment of Foot (later the East Lancashire Regiment) as an ensign. Sartorius was promoted to lieutenant in July 1865, and in June 1869 he was awarded the Royal Humane Society Bronze Medal for saving the lives of three girls at Broadstairs, Kent.

In December 1870 he passed the examination at the Staff College and for four years was an instructor in Military Surveying at Sandhurst. In 1874 he married Emily Cook and they had a son and two daughters. Later in 1874 en-route to rejoining his regiment Sartorius spent some time in Persia.

During the Afghan War Sartorius commanded a company of the 59th which escorted the guns of Battery D/2, Royal Artillery, from Quetta to Kandahar, and afterwards took part in the advance and capture of Kalat-i-Ghilzai in January 1879. Having been promoted to captain, Sartorius commanded the company in October 1879 which took part in the advance of Brigadier General Hughes' forces in Tazi.

On 24 October 1897, at Shahjui, Sartorius led a party of five or six men in a surprise attack on an enemy stronghold in an almost inaccessible position, on the top of a steep hill. They crept up on the picket unawares, until spotted. Sartorius and his men were then fired on as they reached the top of the steep pathway. The position was taken with the loss of only one man.

Lieutenant Irwin later wrote of the incident:

Captain Sartorius ordered his men to fix bayonets, and to clamber up. The hill was very steep and when they got to within a few feet of the top, the Afghans sprang up with a yell and, sword in hand, slashing right and left, simply jumped down upon our fellows. For a few moments all was confusion, friend and foe falling down together, but it was speedily all over. We had gained the hill, and the standards on it, not one of the enemy having escaped. We lost just one man, and Captain Sartorius was wounded in both hands. The fanatics were splendid, though ferocious-looking scoundrels, and fought like fiends, having evidently made up their minds to die, and to do as much damage as possible before doing so.

Sartorius' VC was gazetted on 17 May 1881, and he was presented with it by Queen Victoria at Windsor Castle on 1 July 1881.

Due to his wounds he partially lost the use of his right hand. In 1882 he served in the Egyptian Campaign as Deputy Assistant Adjutant General where he was mentioned in despatches. He retired from the army in 1905 with the rank of major general, but in 1909 he was appointed colonel of the South Lancashire Regiment (Prince of Wales' Volunteers). In January 1915 his wife, Emily, died and in April the same year his son was killed in action.

Euston Sartorius died on 19 February 1925 and is buried in St. Peter & St. Paul Churchyard, Ewhurst, Surrey.

His VC is held by the National Army Museum, London.

His brother Reginald Sartorius was also awarded the VC (page 61).

James William ADAMS
KILLA KAZI
11 December 1879

James William Adams VC

James Adams was born on 24 November 1839 in Cork, Ireland, the only son of Thomas O'Brien Adams, justice of the peace, and Elizabeth Williams. He was educated at Hamlin and Porter's School, Cork, and at Trinity College, Dublin, where he took his Bachelor of Arts degree. Adams was a keen sportsman in athletics and gymnastics; he was also a fine horseman.

Adams was ordained as a deacon in 1863 and a priest in the following year, and was curate to the Reverend Warren at Hyde, Hampshire until 1866.

He wanted to travel to India, where, in October 1866, he became a chaplain on the Bengal Ecclesiastical Establishment, under Bishop Millman, based in Calcutta. Shortly after, Adams contracted a fever and was sent to Ceylon to recuperate. On his recovery he was posted to Peshawar and began to work with the troops stationed there. Adams did a great deal of work during the cholera outbreaks that regularly occurred in the camps.

In 1870 he transferred to Allahabad and was sent on special duty to Kashmir in 1874.

In January 1876, Adams was appointed to Meerut and in December given charge of the Cavalry and Artillery Camp for the Delhi Durbar assemblage, on the occasion of the Prince of Wales' visit. Then, in November 1877, he was summoned to join the Khurram Field Force, and accompanied the Kabul Field Force under Sir Donald Stewart and Sir Frederick Roberts VC, taking part in the march to Kandahar and was present at a number of engagements.

At Killa Kazi, on 11 December 1879, some of the men from the 9th Lancers had fallen from their horses into a wide ditch and were trapped underneath their horses. Well aware from the shouting and firing that the enemy were nearly upon them, Reverend Adams jumped into the water, pulled the men clear of their horses and escaped on foot. He was known by the men as the 'Fighting Parson.'

Lord Roberts VC recommended Adams for the VC but was told it could not be given to him as the award was only for army and Royal Navy personnel. However, in 1881, Queen Victoria signed an amendment to the Royal Warrant allowing members of the ecclesiastical establishment to be eligible for the award and Adams VC was gazetted on 24 August 1881. It was presented to him by Queen Victoria at Windsor Castle on 1 December 1881.

Adams was married to Alice Mary Willshire in August 1881, and they had one daughter. In February 1883 he was sent to Nainital on a two-year appointment, after which he was requested by Lord Roberts VC to accompany the Burma Field Force.

In 1886, after 20 years' service in India, Adams returned to England and became a priest in Postwick, near Norwich, remaining there until 1894 due to ill-health. He spent two years in Jersey, and spent some time working in Wimbotsham, Norfolk. In May 1900 he was appointed honorary chaplain to the Prince of Wales and, following his accession as Edward VII, he was confirmed as honorary chaplain to the King. In 1902 Adams resigned and moved to Ashwell.

Adams died from an acute neuritis on 24 October 1903 and is buried in St. Mary's Churchyard, Church Close, Ashwell, Rutland.

His VC is in The Ashcroft Gallery, Imperial War Museum, London.

A stained glass window was dedicated to him at his church in Stow Bardolph.

Adams is one of only five civilians to be awarded the VC, the others being William McDonell (1857), Thomas Kavanagh (1857), Ross Lowis Mangles (1857) and George Chicken (1858).

William Henry DICK-CUNYNGHAM
SHERPUR PASS
13 December 1879

William Henry Dick-Cunyngham VC

William Dick-Cunyngham was born on 16 June 1851 in Edinburgh, the youngest son of Sir William Hanmer Dick-Cunyngham and Susan Stewart. He was educated at Trinity College, Glenalmond, and at the Royal Military College, Sandhurst. Dick-Cunyngham was gazetted an ensign in the 92nd (Gordon Highlanders) Regiment of Foot (later the Gordon Highlanders) in February 1872, and was promoted to lieutenant in 1873. He set sail with his regiment for India the same year. Dick-Cunyngham was adjutant from January 1877 to April 1878.

During the Afghan War he served in various capacities, firstly in the Transport Department of the Quetta Field Force, and took part in the advance of Sir Donald Stewart's Division on Kandahar. He was present at the actions at Ali Khel, 18 October 1879, in the expedition to Mardan in November, and the operation around Kabul from 8 to 23 December.

On 13 December 1879, during the assault on Takht-i-Shah at the Sherpur Pass, when Lieutenant St. John Forbes and the standard-bearer were hit and the men began to waver under a heavy fire, Lieutenant Dick-Cunyngham rode out in front, exposing himself to the fire, raised his claymore aloft and called on his men to follow him. With a cheer they charged, and the pass was taken.

Dick-Cunyngham served throughout the remainder of the war, seeing action at Childukhtean, 25 April 1880, and took part in the March on Kandahar, being mentioned in despatches on both occasions.

He was sent to South Africa with his regiment to take part in the First Boer War where he was promoted to captain in October 1881.

His VC was gazetted on 18 October 1881, and he was presented with it by Queen Victoria at Windsor Castle on 1 December 1881.

Following the outbreak of the Second Boer War, Lieutenant Colonel Dick-Cunyngham led the 2nd Battalion into battle at Elandslaagte on 21 October 1988, where he was wounded in the leg. His wound incapacitated him during the early part of the Siege of Ladysmith.

On 6 January 1900, almost the first day on which he resumed his active duty and during a great attack on the city, he was killed by a shot from nearly 3,000 yards. He is buried in Ladysmith Cemetery, Natal, South Africa.

His VC is held by the Gordon Highlanders Museum, Aberdeen.

Arthur George HAMMOND
ASMAI HEIGHTS
14 December 1879

Arthur George Hammond VC

Arthur Hammond was born on 28 September 1843 in Dawlish, Devon, the fifth son of Major Thomas John Hammond and Anne (née Warren). He was educated at King Edward VI School, Sherborne, Dorset, and entered the Addiscombe Military Seminary in February 1861. In June of the same year Hammond was commissioned and was posted to India. On his arrival in Calcutta in December he was attached to the 82nd Regiment of Foot (Prince of Wales's Volunteers).

In October 1862 Hammond joined the 12th Native Infantry and, following a successful examination in Hindustani, was posted to the Corps of Guides in September 1863. He was then involved in the Umbeyla Campaign during which he commanded a detachment and held the fort at Mardan. In May 1864 he was made quartermaster of his regiment and, in June 1867, joined the Bengal Staff Corps. Having passed Military Surveying and Field Engineering at Rurki College he served in the Jowaki Campaign of 1877-78, twice being mentioned in despatches.

During the Afghan War, he took part in the storming of Takht-i-Shah on 13 December, and the Asmai Heights on 14 December 1879. Then, Captain Hammond defended the top of the hill, single-handedly, with only a rifle and fixed bayonet against large numbers of Afghans, allowing the 72nd Highlanders and Guides to retire. On his retreat down the hill he stopped to help carry a wounded sepoy when the Afghans were only 60 yards away and firing heavily all the time.

His VC was gazetted on 18 October 1881, and it was presented to him by Queen Victoria at Windsor Castle on 1 December 1881.

In June 1886 he married Edith Jane Wright, and they had three children. Hammond commanded the 3rd Sikhs during the Hazara Campaign of 1888 and was mentioned in despatches. On 12 April 1889 he was awarded the Distinguished Service Order for his actions on the North-West Frontier. Hammond was appointed aide-de-camp to Queen Victoria in 1890. Then he became commandant of the Queen's Own Corps of Guides, a post he held from 1891 to 1895.

In 1897 he was appointed brigadier general of the Assam Brigade and commanded the Peshawar Column and later the 3rd Brigade, Khyber Field Force in the Tirah Campaign of 1897-98.

He died on 20 April 1919 and is buried in St. Michael's Churchyard, London Road, Camberley, Surrey.

His VC is in The Ashcroft Gallery, Imperial War Museum, London.

William John VOUSDEN
<u>ASMAI HEIGHTS</u>
14 December 1879

William John Vousden VC

William Vousden was born on 20 September 1845 in Perth, Scotland, the son of Captain Vousden, late of the 51st Fusiliers. He was educated at Hill's Establishment at Woolwich, and King's School, Canterbury. Vousden entered the army as an ensign in January 1864, joining the 35th Regiment of Foot. In October 1867 he was promoted to lieutenant and transferred to the 5th Punjab Cavalry, and in due course was entered into the Bengal Staff Corps.

Vousden was promoted to captain in January 1876 and served in the two Afridi Campaigns on the staff, and during the Afghan War with his regiment. He was present in the Khort Valley Expedition in January 1879, and took part in the second campaign with Sir Frederick Roberts VC in the advance to Kabul.

On 14 December 1879, at the Asmai Heights, Capt. Vousden charged with a small party into the centre of the retreating Kohistani Force, who outnumbered him greatly. After rapidly charging through, backwards and forwards, cutting down thirty, five of whom he killed himself, Vousden and his party then swept off round the opposite side of a village and joined the rest of the troops.

Vousden was mentioned in despatches three times during the Afghan War and was promoted to brevet major.

His VC was gazetted on 18 October 1881, and he was presented with it by the Lieutenant Governor of Bengal, the Honourable Augustus Rivers Thompson, on 24 May 1882.

Vousden saw service in the Miranzai Expedition, the Tochi Field Force, the Tirah Campaign and the North-West Frontier, during all of which he was mentioned in despatches.

Vousden was married in 1891 to the daughter of Major General Drummond. In 1901, now a major general, he was given command of the Punjab Frontier Force and district.

Vousden died from dysentery on 2 November 1902 and is buried in Lahore Cemetery, Pakistan.

His VC is not publicly held.

His nephew Arthur Borton was also awarded the VC in Palestine in 1917.

George SELLAR
ASMAI HEIGHTS
14 December 1879

George Sellar VC

George Sellar was born in 1850 in Keith, Banffshire, Scotland. He enlisted into the 72nd (The Duke of Albany's Own Highlanders) Regiment of Foot circa 1869.

On 14 December 1879, at the Asmai Heights, Lance Corporal Sellar led the assault under heavy fire, dashing up the slope ahead of his party and engaged in hand-to-hand fighting with an Afghan who sprang out to meet him, whom he defeated despite receiving a knife wound to the arm. His action was observed by none other than Lord Roberts VC, watching through his field glass.

Sellar's VC was gazetted on 18 October 1881, and he was presented with it by the General Officer Commanding Oudh, Lieutenant General Cureton in Lucknow, India on 14 December 1881. His regiment was amalgamated with the 78th (Highlanders) Regiment of Foot to become the 1st Battalion, Seaforth Highlanders and by 1882 Sellar had been promoted to sergeant.

His battalion was shipped to Egypt in 1882 and he fought at Tel-el-Kebir. In 1887 Sellar was appointed sergeant instructor of the Lairg Company of 1st Sutherland and the Caithness Highland Rifle Volunteers.

Sellar died on 1 November 1889 and is buried in Lairg Cemetery, Lairg, Sutherland, Scotland.

His VC is held by the Queen's Own Highlanders Museum, Fort George, Ardersier, Inverness-shire, Scotland.

Patrick MULLANE
MAIWAND
27 July 1880

Patrick Mullane VC

Patrick Mullane was born in October 1858 in Ahmednuggar (now Ahmednagar), Deccan, India. He enlisted into the Royal Horse Artillery in India. He was promoted to sergeant and was posted to serve in the Afghan War with his battery.

On 27 July 1880 at Maiwand, during the retreat to Kandahar, Sergeant Mullane saw Driver Pickwell Istead lying wounded on the ground. Although the enemy were only ten yards away, he sprang from his horse, lifted the mortally wounded man onto the limber of his gun and got him away. Istead subsequently died. Also, during the retreat he entered several villages under heavy fire to get water for the wounded.

His VC was gazetted on 16 May 1881, and he was presented with it by Lord Roberts VC at Poona Racecourse, India on 11 July 1881. Mullane continued to serve in India, rising to the rank of sergeant major by the time of his retirement, with a pension.

In 1904, while he was abroad, his decoration was sold by his family who believed him to be dead; on his return home the decoration was restored to him.

Mullane died on 20 November 1919 and was buried in an unmarked grave in St. Patrick's Roman Catholic Cemetery; St. Matthew's Plot, Row 79, Grave 49, Langthorne Road, Leytonstone, London (the grave has been re-used and now has the name Mary Dore; in 2013 a headstone bearing his name was placed nearby).

His VC is not publicly held.

James COLLIS
MAIWAND
28 July 1880

James Collis VC

James Collis was born on 19 April 1856 in Cambridge. He enlisted into the Royal Horse Artillery and saw service in the Afghan War.

On 28 July 1880 at Maiwand, during the retreat to Kandahar when the officer commanding his battery was endeavouring to bring in a limber, with wounded men under heavy fire, Gunner Collis ran forward and drew the enemy fire onto himself. Later he was seen fetching water, tending to the wounded and maintaining his humour while many died of fatigue on the road. When he saw twelve enemy cavalry approaching, he broke off, lay down in a ravine and opened fire. Thinking that he was several men, the enemy halted and returned fire. He killed two of the enemy before being relieved.

His VC was gazetted on 16 May 1881 and was presented to him by Lord Roberts VC at Poona Racecourse, India on 11 July 1881. Collis was discharged from the army in 1881 and he joined the Bombay Police rising to the rank of inspector. In March 1882 he married the widow Adela Grace Skuse.

In 1887 Collis returned to Britain and re-enlisted into the army, joining the Suffolk Regiment. His regiment was posted to India the following year, but Collis was invalided home suffering from rheumatic fever, leaving his wife in India. In 1893 he married Mary Goddard who was unaware that Collis was still married. In 1895 his deception was discovered, and he was convicted of bigamy and sentenced to 18 months hard labour. Due to his conviction he was the subject of a Forfeiture Warrant signed by the Sovereign, meaning his decoration was to be returned. However he was not struck off the Register of the VC as only the decoration and pension were forfeited.

The practice was discontinued in 1920 when George V was so concerned by the prospect of future forfeits it was declared: 'The King feels so strongly that, no matter the crime committed by anyone on whom the VC has been conferred, the decoration should not be forfeited. Even were a VC [recipient] be sentenced to be hanged for murder, he should be allowed to wear his VC on the scaffold.'

Collis had already pawned his decoration for eight shillings (40p). The decoration was retrieved by the police for the Crown on the instructions of the Home Office. Following a number of jobs he re-enlisted into the Suffolk Regiment as a drill-instructor on the outbreak of the First World War, aged 58. However, he was dogged with ill-health and was again invalided out of the army in August 1917.

Collis died from heart disease on 28 June 1918 and is buried with full military honours in Wandsworth Cemetery; Section 53, Grave 115, Magdalen Road, London. However, his family did not attend the service as they saw him as a black sheep.

The location of his VC was unknown from 1896 until 1938, when it was sold at auction to Colonel Oakley; himself awarded the Military Cross during the First World War. His sister sold the decoration in 1980 and for the next 38 years it was in private ownership. In 2014 the decoration was sold at auction and is now in The Ashcroft Gallery, Imperial War Museum, London.

William St. Lucien CHASE
DEH KHOJA
16 August 1880

William St. Lucien Chase VC

William Chase was born on 2 July 1856 on the island of St. Lucia, in the West Indies, the eldest son of Captain R. H. Chase, Commissary of Ordnance and Susan Hill. He was educated privately, and entered the army in 1875, joining the 15th Regiment of Foot.

Chase was posted to India where he served with the Regimental Headquarters for two years and, on passing his exams with distinction, was admitted into the Bombay Staff Corps. Chase did his duty successfully at Poona, Ahmadabad, Baroda and Surat. During the Afghan War he served with the 28th Bombay Native Infantry and accompanied the headquarters of his regiment as part of the Kandahar Field Force.

Chase was present throughout the defence of Kandahar and took part in the ill-fated sortie to Deh Khoja on 16 August 1880. Lieutenant Colonel Newport and 50 men were killed or wounded. Lieutenant Chase, with Private Thomas Ashford (page 99), went to the aid of Private Massey who had taken cover in a blockhouse and was wounded. Chase and Ashford carried Massey for over 200 yards. Bullets were raising dust all around them and they fell three times but eventually reached safety.

After Chase's regiment left Kandahar he was given command of the

Killa Abdulla Post, until he was relieved in November 1880. Then he was sent to command the post of Gatai, on the lines of communication, remaining there until all the troops of the Kandahar Evacuating Force had passed through en route to India.

Chase's VC was gazetted on 7 October 1881, and he was presented with it by the General Officer Commanding Bombay, at Poona on 23 January 1882.

In 1884 he served in the Zhob Campaign, in the Chin Lushai Expedition, and the advance on Fort Haka. In 1893 he took part in the Naga Hills Campaign and Manipur, in 1897 the Mohmand Expedition, the Tirah campaigns of 1897 and 1898, and was present at the actions of the Sampagha Pass, the occupation of Maiden and Bagh Valley, and operations in the Dwatoi Defile, Rejghul Valley and Bara Valley, being mentioned in despatches numerous times.

Chase later commanded the 28th Bombay Pioneers and was made brevet colonel.

He died on 24 June 1908 and is buried in the English Cemetery, Quetta, Pakistan.

His VC is held by the Army Museum of Western Australia, Fremantle, Australia.

Thomas Elsdon ASHFORD
DEH KHOJA
16 August 1880

Thomas Elsdon Ashford VC

99

Thomas Ashford was born in 1859 in Newmarket, Suffolk. He enlisted into the 2nd Battalion, Royal Fusiliers in 1877 and was posted to Afghanistan.

On 16 August 1880, the 2nd Battalion took part in the ill-fated sortie to Deh Khoja, where Lieutenant Colonel Newport and 50 men were killed or wounded. Lieutenant Chase (page 98) and Private Ashford went to the aid of Private Massey who had taken cover in a blockhouse and was wounded. Chase and Ashford carried Massey for over 200 yards. Bullets were raising dust all around them and they fell three times but eventually they reached safety.

Ashford's VC was gazetted on 7 October 1881, and he was presented with it by Lord Roberts VC at Madras on 13 December 1881.

After his military service he returned to England and took up work as a postman in Thringstone. Ashford married Betsy Ann Sisson on 29 January 1981, and they later moved to Whitwick.

Ashford died from bronchitis on 21 February 1913 and is buried in Whitwick Cemetery, Church Lane, Whitwick, Leicestershire. Despite thousands of mourners attending the service his grave remained unmarked until 1992.

His VC is held by the Royal Fusiliers Museum, Tower of London.

Naga Hills Expedition (1879-80)

Although Britain controlled most of India, the tribal Naga people in the north were turbulent and resisted British rule. In 1879 they murdered a British Commissioner and besieged the garrison at Kohima. A punitive expedition under Brigadier-General John Nation was sent to restore order.

Richard Kirby RIDGEWAY
KONOMA
22 November 1879

Richard Kirby Ridgeway VC

Richard Ridgeway was born on 18 August 1848 in Oldcastle, County Meath, Ireland, the second son of Richard and Anne Ridgway. He was educated privately and later at the Royal Military College, Sandhurst. Ridgway entered the 96th Regiment of Foot as an ensign in January 1868 and was promoted to lieutenant in February 1870.

In 1871 he married Emily Maria (whom he called Amy). The following year he transferred into the Bengal Staff Corps and from 1874 was adjutant of the 44th Gurkha Rifles (later 8th Gurkha Rifles). Ridgway took part in the First Naga Hills Expedition of 1875 during which he was mentioned in despatches.

On 22 November 1879, during the final assault at Konoma, he charged up to a barricade and attempted to tear down the planking surrounding it to affect an entrance. Under very heavy fire the whole time, he was severely wounded in the shoulder.

His VC, gazetted on 11 May 1880, was posted to him in Ireland as his wounds prevented him from travelling to receive it.

In 1883 he passed Staff College and became a deputy assistant quartermaster general in 1884. Ridgway was promoted to major in 1888 and commanded the 44th Gurkha Rifles from 1891-95, during which time he took part in the Manipur Expedition and was promoted to lieutenant colonel. He also served in the Tirah campaign of 1897-98 and retired from the army in 1906.

Ridgeway died from pneumonia on 11 October 1924 and was cremated at Lawnswood Crematorium, his ashes were scattered in the cemetery copse (now cleared), near Columbarium, Leeds.

His VC is not publicly held.

Morosi's Mountain Campaign (1879) & Basuto Gun War (1880-1881)

Basutoland, on the border of Natal, had been a British Protectorate since 1868. in 1871 Britain annexed their land, interfering with the Chiefs' authority and the tribes' traditional law. Resentment grew and in 1879 troops from the Cape were sent to suppress the unrest. Then in 1880 the Cape authorities prepared to enforce the Cape Peace Preservation Act of 1878, which would disarm the natives. This gave rise to the Basuto Gun War.

Robert George SCOTT
MOROSI'S MOUNTAIN
8 April 1879

Robert George Scott VC

Robert Scott was born on 22 April 1874 in Peterborough, the son of Robert Charles and Mary Elizabeth Scott. He was educated at Epsom College and Aberdeen Grammar School, and he joined the Cape Mounted Rifles in September 1876, aged 18. Scott served as a rifleman between 1876 and 1879, taking part in the Anglo-Zulu War.

On 8 April 1879, at Morosi's Mountain, Sgt Scott volunteered to throw time-fused shells as hand grenades over a line of stone barricades, from behind which the enemy were bringing a heavy fire. He made his men take cover in case the shells exploded prematurely. He then crept up to the enemy's position and threw the first bomb over the wall. As he threw the second bomb it exploded as it left his hand, blowing his right hand off and wounding him severely in the leg.

Scott's VC was gazetted on 1 October 1880, and he was presented with it by Queen Victoria at Windsor Castle on 17 December 1880, following which he returned to South Africa where he married Constance Mary in 1884 and they had four children.

Scott was promoted to major and fought in the Second Boer War with the Kimberley Light Horse, being mentioned in despatches and awarded the Distinguished Service Order.

During the First World War, now a lieutenant colonel, Scott commanded the Kimberley Commandos operating on the German South-West Africa border during the Cape Town Rebellion, and later commanded the Veteran Regiment.

Scott died from natural causes on 3 October 1918 and is buried in Plumstead Cemetery; Allotment EA, Grave 88, Wynberg, South Africa.

His VC is not publicly held.

Peter BROWN
MOROSI'S MOUNTAIN
8 April 1879

Peter Brown VC

Peter Brown was born in 1837 in Sweden. He served with the Cape Mounted Rifles during the Basuto War.

On 8 April 1879, at Morosi's Mountain, during the assault the troopers were ordered to take cover when the enemy opened fire. On hearing three wounded men crying for water, Trooper Brown called out, 'I can't stand this any longer, has anyone any water?' Someone gave him a tin and he walked across open ground to the men and began pouring water into their mouths. As he did this, he was hit by a bullet that shattered his arm and another which struck his leg, but he did not stop until the tin was shot through and useless.

His VC was gazetted on 12 April 1880, and he was presented with it by Lord Wolseley at King William's Town later the same year. Brown was invalided out of the Cape Mounted Rifles due to his injuries.

He died from Bright's disease on 11 September 1894 and was buried in an unmarked grave in Woltemade Cemetery; Grave 81594A (although Brown is still buried there, the grave has since been re-used, and bears the name Abrahamse), Cape Town, South Africa.

His VC is held by the Amathole Museum, King William's Town, South Africa.

Edmund Barron HARTLEY
MOROSI'S MOUNTAIN
5 June 1879

Edmund Barron Hartley VC

Edmund Hartley was born on 6 May 1847 in Ivybridge, Devon, the eldest son of Doctor Edmund Hartley and received his medical education at St. George's Hospital, London. Prior to this he had worked as a clerk in HM Inland Revenue from 1867-69.

In 1874 Hartley travelled to South Africa and was soon appointed district surgeon of British Basutoland, being the first English medical man in that country. He remained there until 1877, when native wars broke out along the south-eastern frontiers of the Cape Colony. He volunteered for service, being appointed surgeon of the Frontier Armed Mounted Police (soon to be renamed the Cape Mounted Rifles).

His first experience of warfare was as medical officer of a column composed of the Naval Brigade, 1st Battalion, 24th Regiment of Foot (later the South Wales Borderers) and the Connaught Rangers (88th Regiment of Foot). They were operating against the Galeeka tribe.

The following year came the Gaika Campaign, when he was appointed principal medical officer of the Cape Town Colonial Forces, a post he held until 1903.

On 5 June 1879, at Morosi's Mountain, Surgeon Major Hartley crossed open ground under heavy fire and carried Corporal Johns to safety. He then returned under fire in order to dress the wounds of the other wounded men; this he did throughout the day.

His VC was gazetted on 7 October 1881, and he was presented with it by Brigadier General Charles Mansfield Clarke on 3 December 1881. Colonel Hartley was General Gordon's principal medical officer for ten months during 1882-83. In 1897 he served in the Bechuanaland Rebellion during which he was slightly wounded while dressing the wounds of a mortally wounded officer. Hartley served throughout the Second Boer War and retired in 1903.

During his retirement he was commandant of six Voluntary Aid Detachments in Somerset between 1910 and 1912, and during the First World War he was Secretary of the Volunteer Aid Hospital, Seaton, Devon.

He died on 20 March 1919 and is buried in Brookwood Cemetery: St. Judes Avenue, Plot 2, Grave 193293. Cemetery Pales, Woking, Surrey.

His VC is held by the Museum of Military Medicine, Keogh Barracks, Aldershot, Surrey.

Francis FITZPATRICK
SEKUKUNI'S TOWN
28 November 1879

Francis Fitzpatrick was born in December 1859 in Tullycorbet, County Monaghan. He enlisted into the 94th Regiment of Foot (later the Connaught Rangers) just before the outbreak of the Basuto War.

On 28 November 1879, at Sekukuni's Town, Private Fitzpatrick with Private Thomas Flawn (page 107) and six men from the Native Contingent were carrying Lieutenant James Dewar, who was wounded. Suddenly, thirty of the enemy appeared in pursuit. The six natives fled, leaving the two privates to alternate between carrying Dewar and firing into the pursuers, until the wounded officer was brought to safety.

Fitzpatrick's VC was gazetted on 24 February 1880, and he was presented with it by Lieutenant Colonel Philip Robert Anstruther-Lydenburg on 17 September 1881 in the Transvaal while serving in the First Boer War. However, he lost his decoration at Bronkers Spruit, and an official replacement was issued in June 1881. The original decoration was later found and returned to the War Office in August 1881.

Fitzpatrick returned to England briefly in 1882, before transferring to the Duke of Cornwell's Light Infantry, in which he served until he was discharged in May 1888.

He died in poverty on 10 July 1933 and was buried in St. Kentigern's Cemetery; Section 9, Lair 1799, Glasgow.

His VC is held by the National Army Museum, London.

Thomas FLAWN
SEKUKUNI'S TOWN
28 November 1879

Thomas Flawn VC

Thomas Flawn was born on 22 December 1857 in Finedon, near Irthlingborough, Northamptonshire, the son of farm hand Thomas and Fanny Flawn. He was educated at the local church school, before enlisting into the 25th Regiment of Foot in October 1876. He spent the next few years jumping from one regiment to another in order to fight, until in 1879 he volunteered for the 94th Regiment of Foot (later the Connaught Rangers) serving in the later part of the Anglo-Zulu War, after which the regiment took part in the Basuto War.

On 28 November 1879, at Sekukuni's Town, Private Flawn with Private Fitzpatrick (page 106) and six men from the Native Contingent were carrying Lieutenant James Dewar, who was wounded. Suddenly, thirty of the enemy appeared in pursuit. The six natives fled, leaving the two privates to alternate between carrying Dewar and firing into the pursuers, until the wounded officer was brought to safety.

Flawn's VC was gazetted on 24 February 1880, and he was presented with it by Lieutenant Colonel Philip Robert Anstruther-Lydenburg on 17 September 1881 in the Transvaal while serving in the First Boer War.

Flawn returned to England in 1882 and left the army to marry the daughter of William Barley, but she died young. He was remarried to the daughter of Richard Oakley.

Flawn died on 19 January 1925 and is buried in Plumstead Cemetery; Section K 1, Grave 758, Cemetery Road, London.

His VC was sold at auction in 1999 to an unknown buyer for £70,000.

John Frederick McCREA
TWEEFONTEIN
14 January 1881

John Frederick McCrea VC

John McCrea was born on 2 April 1854 in St. Peter Port, Guernsey, Channel Islands, the son of Captain Herbert Taylor McCrea and Elizabeth Dobree Carey. Following the death of his parents in 1855 he was brought up by his aunt Charlotte and was educated at Elizabeth College. McCrea qualified in medicine in 1878 as a member of the Royal College of Surgeons of England and Scotland.

In 1879 McCrea went to South Africa where he worked in the

Military Hospital at Cape Town as a civilian surgeon to Her Majesty's Forces. The following year he moved to the Eastern Cape to settle, but instead volunteered for 1st Cape Mounted Yeomanry as a surgeon and marched into Basutoland in August 1880.

On 14 January 1881, at Tweefontein, after an enemy charge which resulted in 37 casualties, Surgeon McCrea and Captain Buxton went to the rescue of Burgher Aircamp, who was wounded, and they took him to cover. Then, McCrea went to find a stretcher, at which point he was wounded in the chest. McCrea dressed his own wound and then helped the wounded man, and throughout the remainder of the day attended to wounded men under fire. Had it not been for his devotion to duty, there would undoubtedly have been much higher losses.

He was promoted to surgeon major, and his VC was gazetted on 28 June 1881. He was presented with it by Brigadier General Charles Mansfield Clarke at King William Town, Natal on 25 October 1881.

McCrea died from heart failure on 16 July 1894 and is buried in Kokstad Cemetery, Transkei District, Cape Province, South Africa.

His VC is in The Ashcroft Gallery, Imperial War Museum, London.

Anglo-Egyptian War (1882)

Egypt was under the control of the Ottoman Empire. The Sultan forbade the Khedive (Viceroy of Egypt under Turkish rule) to impose any taxes, a policy which spelled financial disaster. But with the opening of the Suez Canal in 1869, influence in Egypt took on a new significance, and Disraeli's government was quick to buy up the Khedive's shares in the canal in 1875. By 1878, the country was virtually bankrupt and, to protect their interest in the canal, England and France took joint control of Egypt's finances, effectively running the country.

With nationalist feelings running high against the Khedive for allowing this, the Egyptian Minister of War, Ahmed Arabi, led a revolt against this interference in May 1882. The Khedive tried to dismiss Arabi and rioting broke out in Alexandra with 50 Europeans being killed. British protests about Arabi's fortifying of the forts came to nothing, so British ships started bombarding the city and harbour.

Israel HARDING
ALEXANDRIA
11 July 1882

Israel Harding VC

Israel Harding was born on 21 October 1833 in Portsmouth, Hampshire, the son of John Harding, a Queen's Pilot at Portsmouth, and Sophia Martin. He was educated at the Royal Victoria School, Portsmouth. Harding served as a cabin boy on his father's ship, the *Echo,* from the age of 14, and enlisted into the Royal Navy in 1849, being assigned to HMS *Arrogant,* but was soon undergoing gunnery training at HMS *Excellent.* In 1853, while still serving at HMS *Excellent,* he married Harriet Ellis, and they had three children.

Harding served onboard HMS *Cressy* during the Crimean War, and later took part in the 1862 expedition to Mexico and the occupation of Vera Cruz. In 1871 while serving onboard HMS *Gladiator* he was awarded the Brazilian Order and given a testimonial from Princess Imperial Regent of Brazil on behalf of Emperor Dom Pedro II for extinguishing a fire at the Arsenal of War in Rio de Janeiro. He also saw action during the Ashanti Wars while serving aboard HMS *Victor Emanuel* as a gunner. In 1873 he divorced Harriet on the grounds of adultery, and the following year married Emma Annette (née Nunn), with whom he had four daughters.

On 11 July 1882, at Alexandria, HMS *Alexandra* with other ships was bombarding the forts of the city, when a 10-inch shell penetrated the side armour and rolled along the deck, ending up near the hatchway leading to the magazine. Gunner Harding, on hearing the shouts from the men rushed up from below, picked up the still burning shell and flung it into a tub of water.

His VC was gazetted on 15 September 1882, and he was presented with it by the Commander-in-Chief Malta, Lord Alcester on 14 November. Harding's second wife, Emma, died in 1912 and, although over 80, he served in the First World War.

Harding died from cerebral thrombosis on 11 May 1917 and is buried in Highland Road Cemetery: Section H, Grave 7-59, Highland Road, Southsea, Portsmouth, Hampshire.

His VC is in The Ashcroft Gallery, Imperial War Museum, London.

Frederick CORBETT (real name David EMBLETON)
KAFR DOWAR
5 August 1882

Frederick Corbett VC

David Embleton was born on 17 September 1853 in Camberwell, London. He enlisted under the name of Frederick Corbett into the King's Royal Rifles Corps in 1873 and was posted to Egypt with the 3rd Battalion in 1882.

On 5 August 1882, at Kafr Dowar, during a reconnaissance Lieutenant Howard Vyse was mortally wounded and lying in the open. There being no time to move him, Private Corbett asked and was given permission to remain with him and, although under constant fire, he at once tried to stop the bleeding. When ordered to retreat he helped carry the officer from the field.

His VC was gazetted on 16 February 1883, and he was presented it by the Commander-in-Chief Gibraltar, Lord Napier, in Cairo on 2 March 1884. Following his discharge from the army, Cobbett sold his VC.

He subsequently re-enlisted into the Royal Artillery, but Corbett went absent without leave (AWOL) from 12 to 23 July 1884 and was arrested, charged with being AWOL, theft and embezzling money belonging to an officer. He was found guilty.

Corbett is one of eight men to forfeit his VC. Due to his conviction he was the subject of a Forfeiture Warrant signed by the Sovereign, meaning his decoration was to be returned. However, he was not struck off the Register of the VC, as only the decoration and pension were forfeited.

The practice was discontinued in 1920 when George V was so concerned by the prospect of future forfeits it was declared: 'The King feels so strongly that, no matter the crime committed by anyone on whom the VC has been conferred, the decoration should not be forfeited. Even were a VC [recipient] be sentenced to be hanged for murder, he should be allowed to wear his VC on the scaffold.'

Corbett fell on hard times and ended up in a workhouse, where he died from brain cancer on 25 September 1912. He is buried in London Road Cemetery (also known as Maldon Cemetery); Row 4, Grave 27, Maldon, Essex.

His VC is held by the Royal Green Jackets Museum, Winchester, Hampshire.

William Mordaunt Marsh EDWARDS
TEL-EL-KEBIR
13 September 1882

William Mordaunt Marsh Edwards VC

William Edwards was born on 7 May 1855 in Hardingham, Norfolk, the son of William Henry Bartholomew Edwards and Caroline Marsh. He was educated privately at Rottingdean, Eton, and at Trinity College, Cambridge. Gazetted a second lieutenant in March 1876, he joined the 74th (Highland) Regiment of Foot. He served in the Straits Settlements and Hong Kong. In 1881 the 74th amalgamated with the 71st (Highland) Regiment of Foot to become the Highland Light Infantry and Edwards was posted to Egypt the following year with the 2nd Battalion.

On 13 September 1882, at Tel-el-Kebir, Lieutenant Edwards led his men storming a redoubt. He charged ahead and dashed alone into the enemy battery, killing the officer in charge. Edwards was knocked down by an enemy gunner and about to be killed when his men arrived, saving him.

His VC was gazetted on 13 February 1883, and he was presented with it eleven days later by Queen Victoria at Windsor Castle. Edwards served in India from 1884 to 1887; he was promoted to captain in 1887 and was adjutant of the 3rd Battalion for five years. In November 1889 he married Alice Norton, and they had a son in 1891. Edwards retired from the army in 1896 and in 1899 was appointed to Her Majesty's

Honourable Corps of Gentlemen-at-Arms. He was commissioned as a duty lieutenant of the county of Norfolk in August 1900.

Edwards died on 17 September 1912 and is buried in St. George's Churchyard, Hardingham, Norfolk.

His VC is in The Ashcroft Gallery, Imperial War Museum, London.

First Sudan Campaign (1881-85)

In 1881 the political situation in Sudan was descending into chaos. General Gordon had resigned as governor general and, as his successor was receiving no direction from the government in Cairo, he soon lost control. The slave trade returned, the army was woefully under resourced, and taxes were getting higher and higher.

It was in this atmosphere that the self-styled Mahdi, or 'Guide', gathered the support of Islamic fanatics. A full scale revolt led to the Mahdi's forces controlling most of the country. When Britain had occupied Egypt, it had also taken on the responsibility for the Sudan, and it became evident that military action would be necessary to suppress the revolt.

Arthur Knyvet WILSON
EL TEB,
29 February 1884

Arthur Knyvet Wilson VC

114

Arthur Wilson was born on 4 March 1842 in Swaffham, Norfolk, the son of Rear Admiral George Knyvet Wilson. He entered the Royal Navy as a midshipman in 1855 and served onboard HMS *Algiers* during the Crimean War. He transferred to HMS *Raleigh* and after her loss served onboard HMS *Calcutta* during the Third China War, seeing action with the Naval Brigade at the Battle of Canton and the Taku Forts. Wilson was promoted to lieutenant in December 1861 and in 1865 joined the gunnery school at HMS *Excellent*, Portsmouth.

Wilson became an instructor at the new Imperial Japanese Naval Academy at Yokohama in May 1867 and then at the new training ship HMS *Britannia* in January 1869. The following year he became a member of the committee investigating the effectiveness of the Whitehead torpedo, and in 1876 he was appointed commander of the new torpedo school at HMS *Vernon*, where his duties included rewriting torpedo manuals, inverting aiming apparatus and developing mine warfare. Wilson was an advocate of the torpedo, but a committed opponent of the submarine, describing it as 'A damned un-English weapon.'

Wilson was promoted to captain in April 1880 and given command of the depot ship HMS *Hecla*. In the summer of 1882 the *Hecla* was ordered to Egypt to deliver ammunition for British troops. On arrival, with the help of Captain John Fisher, he installed a heavy gun on a railway carriage and used it as an improvised armoured train. In early 1884 the *Hecla* was ordered to the Sudan to support British troops.

On 29 February 1884, at El Teb, Captain Wilson attached himself (he later said he had nothing else to do that day) to the right half-battery of the Naval Brigade, in place of a lieutenant who was mortally wounded. As the troops closed in on the enemy's Krupp battery, the Arabs charged the gunners before they could deploy the guns. Wilson sprang to the front and attacked an Arab, his sword stuck in the man's ribs and snapped in two. He fought on with his fists and was slashed across the head, before being relieved by men from the York and Lancaster Regiment. His action protected the gunners, so they were able to deploy their guns.

His VC was gazetted on 21 May 1884, and he was presented with it by the Commander-in-Chief Portsmouth, Admiral Sir George Phipps-Hornby, in Portsmouth on 6 June 1884. He was aide-de-camp to Queen Victoria 1892-95, and Lord Commissioner of the Admiralty and Controller of the Navy 1897-1901. From 1901 to 1903 Wilson was in command of the Channel Squadron, and from 1903 to 1907 was Commander-in-Chief of the Home and Channel Fleets. He was appointed First Lord of the Admiralty in 1909 and held the post until he retired in 1912.

Wilson died on 25 May 1921 and is buried in St. Peter & St. Paul Churchyard, Swaffham, Norfolk.

His VC is held by the National Museum of the Royal Navy, Portsmouth.

William Thomas MARSHALL
EL TEB
29 February 1884

William Thomas Marshall VC

William Marshall was born on 5 December 1854 in Newark, Nottinghamshire, the son of John Richard Marshall. He was educated privately and joined the 19th Hussars in July 1873. Marshall took part in the Egyptian War of 1882-84, being present at the Battle of Tel-el-Kebir, following which he was sent to Sudan.

On 29 February 1884, at El Teb, the 19th Hussars commanding officer, Lieutenant Colonel Percy Barrow, was severely wounded during the charge, his horse being killed, and leaving him lying on the ground surrounded by the enemy. Quartermaster Sergeant Marshall, who had stayed behind with him, seized his hand and dragged him through the midst of the enemy and back to the regiment, thus saving him from certain death.

Marshall's VC was gazetted on 21 May 1884, and he was presented with it by Queen Victoria at Windsor Castle on 3 July 1884. He was commissioned a quartermaster in January 1885, and served in the Second Boer War, seeing action at Lombard's Kop, the defence of Ladysmith and Laing's Nek.

Marshall married Louisa Wiseman in October 1900 and they had a daughter. He became camp quartermaster at Aldershot in 1905 and retired in 1907. He became Secretary of the Fife County Territorial Force Association in March 1908. Marshall was mentioned in despatches for his services during the First World War and was promoted to lieutenant colonel in January 1919.

Marshall died on 11 September 1920 and is buried in Bennochy Road Cemetery; Lair 23, Bennochy Road, Kirkcaldy, Fife.

His VC is held by the Light Dragoons Museum, Newcastle-upon-Tyne.

Percival Scrope MARLING
TAMAI
13 March 1884

Percival Scrope Marling VC

Percival Marling was born on 6 March 1861 in Stroud, Gloucestershire, the oldest son of Sir William Henry Marling, Baronet of Stanley Park, Stroud. He was educated at Harrow and the Royal Military College,

Sandhurst. In August 1880 Marling was gazetted a second lieutenant in the 3rd Battalion, 60th Rifles, and served throughout the First Boer War.

Promoted to lieutenant in July 1882, he took part in the Egyptian Campaign, seeing action at Tel-el-Mahuta, Kassassin and Tel-el-Kebir. Marling then went on to serve in Sudan with the Mounted Infantry.

On 13 March 1884, at Tamai, when Private Morley of the Royal Sussex Regiment was wounded, Lieutenant Marling lifted the wounded man onto the saddle in front of him. But Morley immediately fell off, so Marling dismounted as the enemy were closing in and carried him for 800 yards under fire to safety. Unfortunately, Morley died the following day.

His VC was gazetted on 21 May 1884, and he was presented with it by the General Officer Commanding Egypt, General Sir Frederick Charles Arthur Stephenson, in July 1884 in Cairo.

Marling took part in the Nile Expedition with the Camel Corps for the relief of General Gordon where he was present at the fighting in the Bayuda Desert, both actions at Abu Kru, El Gubat and Metemmeh. In October 1885 he was made a local captain and given command of a company of Mounted Infantry in Egypt, which he commanded until February 1887.

In 1889 he proceeded to India as captain with the 18th Hussars and, except for a year when he was adjutant of the West Somerset Yeomanry, he served in India until 1895. In August 1896 he was promoted to major and selected to command the regimental depot at Canterbury, a post he held for two years. In May 1890, now a colonel, Marling married Beatrice Caroline Beaumont.

In June 1899 Marling rejoined the 18th Hussars in Africa and fought at Talana Hill, Lombard's Kop, and during the defence of Ladysmith, but was invalided home in June 1900 suffering with enteric fever. Marling was well enough to return to South Africa in February 1901, and commanded his regiment in the field until May 1902, during operations in the Transvaal, the Orange River Colony and the Zulu Frontier of Natal.

Promoted to brevet colonel in 1905, Marling was given command of the York Garrison and District. In 1909 he was made a temporary brigadier-general in South Africa but had to retire in the following year due to injuries received by his horse falling on top of him while on duty. On the outbreak of the First World War Marling volunteered for duty and in September 1914 went to France and served on the Headquarters Staff of the Indian Army Corps until 1915, when he was invalided home with congestion of the lungs.

He returned to his estate, where he became a justice of the peace and the duty lieutenant. He was also a county councillor for Bristol. He is the author of *Rifleman and Hussar.*

Marling died on 29 May 1936 and is buried in a vault in All Saints Church, Selsley, near Stroud, Gloucestershire.

His VC is in The Ashcroft Gallery, Imperial War Museum, London.

Thomas EDWARDS
TAMAI
13 March 1884

Thomas Edwards VC

Thomas Edwards was born on 19 April 1863 in Brill, Buckinghamshire. When he was 17 years of age he enlisted into the army, and after training was assigned to the 1st Battalion, 42nd (Royal Highland) Regiment of Foot (later the Black Watch) in August 1881. He would serve with this regiment for up to seven years in Africa, including both the Egyptian Campaigns and the Sudan Campaign.

On 13 March, at Tamai, Private Edwards was attached to a naval gun team responsible for the ammunition mules, when No. 4 gun was attacked by a large enemy force, and most of the crew were killed. Edwards took charge, bayoneted two Arabs and shot another who had just cut through the arm of an officer. He defended the gun throughout the action, saving the remaining crew, the ammunition and mules, despite being wounded several times himself.

His VC was gazetted on 21 May 1884. As there is no record of an investiture the decoration may have been posted to him. Edwards continued to serve in Egypt for more than two years until he was posted to Malta with his regiment and from there back to England. In 1892 he was transferred to the reserve; despite his good conduct he remained a private throughout his career.

After leaving the army he settled in York, got married and had two children. In later life he moved to Essex. Edwards died from bronchitis on 27 March 1952 and is buried in an unmarked grave at St. Mary's Churchyard, Chigwell High Road, Chigwell, Essex. In 2001 a headstone was placed near the entrance to the churchyard as the exact location of his grave is not known.

His VC is held by the Black Watch Museum, Balhousie Castle, Perth, Scotland.

Alfred SMITH
ABU KLEA
17 January 1885

Alfred Smith VC

Alfred Smith was born in 1861 in London. He enlisted as a gunner in the Royal Regiment of Artillery.

On 17 January 1885, at Abu Klea, when Lieutenant Guthrie, who had no weapon in his hand, was attacked by a native with a spear. Smith went to his rescue and warded off the spearman with a handspike, giving Guthrie time to draw his sword and bring the assailant to his knees. In the ensuing struggle, the assailant managed to stab Guthrie in the leg with a long knife before Smith killed him with the handspike. Guthrie died of his wounds a few days later.

Smith's VC was gazetted (incorrectly as Albert Smith) on 12 May 1885 and he was presented with it by the General Officer Commanding Egypt, General Sir Frederick Charles Arthur Stephenson, on 3 August 1885.

Smith died in his sleep on 6 January 1932 and is buried in Plumstead Cemetery; Section N, Grave 885, Cemetery Road, Plumstead, London.

His VC is held by the Royal Artillery Museum, Larkhill, Wiltshire.

3

1888 - 1895

Karen-Ni Expedition (1888-89) & Chin Field Force (1889)

Following the British victory in the Third Anglo-Burmese War, many of the natives refused to accept the authority of the occupying British Army and resorted to guerrilla action. They were led mainly by former officers of the disbanded Burmese Royal Army, village headmen and some royal princes. Two punitive expeditions were needed to crush the rebels.

John CRIMMIN
LWEKAW
1 January 1889

John Crimmin VC

John Crimmin was born on 19 March 1859 in Kilballyowen, County Limerick, Ireland. He studied medicine, becoming Licentiate of the

Royal College of Physicians, Licentiate of the Royal College of Surgeons and Doctor of Public Health in Ireland, before entering the Bombay Medical Service in 1882. Crimmin served in Burma from 1886 to 1889 with the Karene Field Force as senior medical officer.

On 1 January 1889 at Lwekaw, Lieutenant Tighe and four men charged into a large body of the enemy who were moving off from the Karen left flank, and two men were wounded. Surgeon Crimmin ran out to attend to the wounded men in the midst of a skirmish with bullets flying all around him. Crimmin then joined the firing line which had by then come up. Then, shortly afterwards they were engaged in driving the bandits away from small clumps of trees in which the enemy took shelter. Crimmin was attending to a wounded man near one of these clumps of trees, when he was attacked by several bandits. Crimmin jumped to his feet and ran his sword through one of the assailants and engaged boldly with another causing them to flee into the bush.

His VC was gazetted on 17 September 1889, and he was presented with it by the Commander-in-Chief Bombay, the Duke of Connaught, later that year in India. Crimmin was promoted to major in 1894, and lieutenant colonel in 1902. He was appointed civil surgeon at Rutnagberry and health officer for the Port of Bombay. In October 1913 he was promoted to colonel.

Crimmin died on 20 February 1945 and is buried in Wells Cemetery; Section F-D-3, Grave 274, Wells, Somerset.

His VC is not publicly held.

Ferdinand Simeon Le QUESNE
TARTAN
4 May 1889

Ferdinand Simeon Le Quesne VC

Ferdinand Le Quesne was born on 25 December 1863 in St. Helier, Jersey, the third son of Lieutenant Colonel N. Le Quesne of the Royal Jersey Artillery and Augusta W. Simeon. He was educated in the Channel Islands and at King's College Hospital, London, before joining the army as a surgeon in July 1886. Le Quesne served in the 1889 Burma Expedition with the medical staff (later the Royal Army Medical Corps).

On 4 May 1889, at Tartan, while part of the Chin Field Force, during the attack on the enemy stockade Surgeon Le Quesne dressed the wounds of a mortally wounded officer for a full ten minutes under steady fire only five yards from the enemy position. He was later wounded while dressing the wounds of another officer.

His VC was gazetted on 29 October 1889 and presented by Major General Sir J. Gordon in Rangoon on 18 January 1890. He served with the Chin Lushai Field Force later in 1890 and with the Wuntho Field Force in 1891. In 1898 he was promoted to major. Le Quesne served in the Second Boer War and was promoted to lieutenant colonel in 1906. Following his retirement in 1918 he settled in the West Country.

Le Quesne died on 14 April 1950 and is buried in Canford Cemetery; Section K, Grave 9, Canford Lane, Bristol, Avon.

His VC is held by the Jersey Museum, St. Helier, Jersey, Channel Islands.

Anglo-Manipur (1891)

Manipur was a small hill state lying between Assam and Burma on India's north-east border. In September 1890 the Raja of Manipur was ousted in a palace coup and the British Government in India saw this as a rebellion. In March of 1891 an expedition was sent to crush it.

Charles James William GRANT
THOBAL
21 March to 9 April 1891

Charles James William Grant VC

Charles Grant was born on 14 October 1861 in Bourtie, Aberdeenshire, Scotland, the son of Lieutenant General PCS St John Grant and Helen, daughter of Colonel William Birset. He was educated privately and later at the Royal Military College, Sandhurst. Grant joined the Suffolk Regiment in May 1882, and the Madras Staff Corps in May 1884, before taking part in the Burma Expedition of 1885-87.

When the Manipur Rebellion started Lieutenant Grant was serving in the Indian Staff Corps and commanded a detachment of the 43rd Gurkha Rifles (later the 8th Gurkha Rifles) stationed on the border post of Tamu, some 55 miles from Manipur.

On hearing of the rebellion he immediately volunteered to attempt the relief of the British captives with just 80 native troops. He reached Thobal, 15 miles from Manipur, on 21 March 1891, stormed the village, took it and immediately entrenched himself. The next day the enemy advanced in great numbers but, without waiting for their attack, Grant with 40 men went out to meet them, formed up and opened fire. For the following nine days his men repulsed repeated attacks. Grant kept the initiative by sallying out whenever possible to attack the Manipuri. They inflicted heavy casualties on the enemy and demoralised them. A relief force joined him on 9 April; Grant had lost one man killed and four were wounded, including himself twice.

For this action he was awarded the VC, gazetted on 26 May 1891, and was presented with it by the Governor of Manipur, Lord Wenlock at Ootacamund, India on 6 July 1891.

He was then appointed aide-de-camp to Lieutenant General Sir James Charlemagne Dormer, Commander-in-Chief, Madras and got married in the same year.

Grant retired from the army with the rank of brevet colonel in 1913.

He died on 23 November 1932 and is buried in Sidmouth Cemetery; Section O, Grave 40, Sidmouth, Devon.

His VC was sold at auction in 2011 for £230,000 to a private buyer. In 2021 it came up for sale again and sold for £420,000 and is now in The Ashcroft Gallery, Imperial War Museum, London.

Hunza-Nagar Campaign (1891)

In 1891, following tribal unrest in the Hunza-Nagar region of India, an expedition was sent to the mountain region to storm the fort at Nilt.

Fenton John AYLMER
NILT FORT
2 December 1891

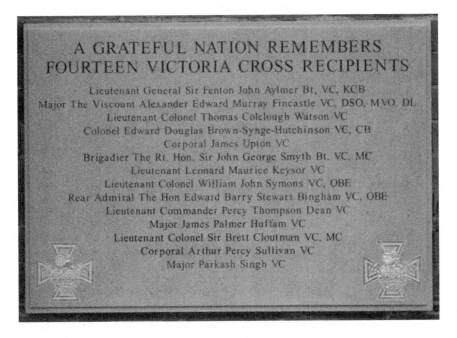

A GRATEFUL NATION REMEMBERS
FOURTEEN VICTORIA CROSS RECIPIENTS

Lieutenant General Sir Fenton John Aylmer Bt, VC, KCB
Major The Viscount Alexander Edward Murray Fincastle VC, DSO, MVO, DL
Lieutenant Colonel Thomas Colclough Watson VC
Colonel Edward Douglas Brown-Synge-Hutchinson VC, CB
Corporal James Upton VC
Brigadier The Rt. Hon. Sir John George Smyth Bt. VC, MC
Lieutenant Leonard Maurice Keysor VC
Lieutenant Colonel William John Symons VC, OBE
Rear Admiral The Hon Edward Barry Stewart Bingham VC, OBE
Lieutenant Commander Percy Thompson Dean VC
Major James Palmer Huffam VC
Lieutenant Colonel Sir Brett Cloutman VC, MC
Corporal Arthur Percy Sullivan VC
Major Parkash Singh VC

Fenton John Aylmer VC

Fenton Aylmer was born on 5 April 1862 in Hastings, Sussex, the second son of Captain Fenton John Aylmer of the 97th Regiment of Foot (who was killed in action just four days after the birth of his son), and Isabella Eleanor Darling. He was educated privately and joined the Royal Engineers as a gentleman cadet in 1880. Fenton served in the Burma Expedition of 1885-87 and the Hazara Expedition of 1891, being mentioned in despatches for the former.

On 2 December 1891, at the Nilt Fort, it being impossible to bring up the guns to bombard the fort, it was decided to take it by storm. Captain Aylmer, with a party of Gurkhas commanded by Lieutenants Boisragon (page 129) and Badcock, hacked away at the abatis and forced an entrance. Then the three officers forced open the outer gate. While Boisragon went back under heavy fire to bring up more men, Aylmer, with total coolness, placed gun cotton (an alternative to gunpowder) on the inner gate and lit the fuse, at which point he was shot in the leg. Having retired to await the explosion, it failed to ignite so he returned to relight it, this time being hit on the hand by a rock dropped from above. After the explosion, he dashed through the gate and engaged the enemy hand-to-hand, killing several with his revolver, until he collapsed from loss of blood.

His VC was gazetted on 12 July 1892, and he was presented with it by the General Officer Commanding Rawalpindi and promoted to major the following year. Aylmer took part in the Isazai Expedition of 1892 and the Chitral Expedition of 1895, being mentioned in despatches and promoted to brevet colonel. In the same year Aylmer saved the life of a drowning man.

In June 1915 Aylmer was promoted to lieutenant general and posted to Mesopotamia where, upon his arrival, he was given command of the Tigris Corps (20,000 men) to affect the relief of Kut.

He set out in December 1915 and arrived at Sheikh Sa'ad. On 6 January 1916 he ordered a direct assault on the Ottoman positions. After two days of fighting the enemy withdrew, Aylmer's force suffered 4,000 casualties. The Ottoman Army under the command of Baron von der Goltz took up positions near the Suwaikiya Marches where, on 13 January Aylmer attacked (Battle of Wadi). The position was carried but with 1,600 casualties. Now reinforced, Aylmer pushed forward to Hanna, where, on 21 January he attacked the Ottoman defences. The Ottomans held their position and inflicted 2,700 casualties on the attackers.

Reinforced again, and with time running out for the garrison at Kut, Aylmer launched a two pronged assault on 7 March 1916 on the Sinn Abtar Redoubt and the Dujaila Redoubt. Intended to be a simultaneous assault, everything went wrong, and the attacks went in piecemeal, the British suffering 4,000 men killed or wounded.

Enough was enough, Aylmer was replaced and would never command in battle again, although he did serve as a divisional commander in India.

He retired from the army in 1919 and was commandant of the Royal Engineers from 1922 until his death.

Aylmer died on 3 September 1935 and his ashes were scattered at Golders Green Crematorium, Hoop Lane, London.

His VC is held by the Royal Engineers Museum, Gillingham, Kent.

Guy Hudleston **BOISRAGON**
NILT FORT
2 December 1891

Guy Hudleston Boisragon VC

Guy Boisragon was born on 5 November 1864 in Kohat, India (now Pakistan), the eldest son of Major General Henry M. Boisragon and Anna Hudleston. He was sent to England for his education at Charterhouse, and later at the Royal Military College, Sandhurst.

Boisragon joined the 10th Regiment of Foot (later the Lincolnshire Regiment) in 1885 but transferred into the 5th Gurkha Rifles in 1887. He took part in both the Hazara Expeditions of 1889 and 1891. Boisragon also served in both Miranzai Expeditions of 1891, the first of these as orderly officer to the general officer commanding.

On 2 December 1891, Boisragon led the assault on the outer gate at the Nilt Fort but, finding his force insufficient, he went back under heavy crossfire to get more men to relieve the first party. He then fought his way to the inner gate which was forced open by Captain Aylmer (page 127) using gun cotton (an alternative to gunpowder). It was largely due to the actions of these men that the fort was taken.

Boisragon's VC was gazetted on 12 July 1892 and presented to him later the same year while still in India. He next saw service in the Waziristan Campaign of 1894-95 under Sir William Lockhart, and then was aide-de-camp to the lieutenant general of the Punjab. In 1896 he was promoted to captain and in 1897 and 1898 took part in operations in the Samana and Kurram Valley. His last service of the 19th century was in the 1897-98 Tirah Campaign.

Promoted to major in 1903, he was a brevet colonel and later colonel of the Frontier Force. Boisragon also served in the First World War, being wounded. Following the war he retired to the south of France with the rank of brigadier.

Boisragon died on 14 July 1931 and is buried in Kensal Green Cemetery; Square 119, Row 2, Grave 18585, London.

His VC is not publicly held.

John MANNERS-SMITH
NILT
20 December 1891

John Manners-Smith VC

John Manners-Smith was born on 30 August 1864 in Lahore, India (now Pakistan), the fifth son of Charles Manners-Smith, Fellow of the Royal College of Surgeons, and Surgeon General of the Indian Medical Service. He was educated at Trinity College, Stratford-upon-Avon, King Edward VI School, Norwich, and the Royal Military College, Sandhurst.

Manners-Smith was promoted to lieutenant in 1883 in the Norfolk Regiment, and in 1885 he joined the Indian Staff Corps and served with the 2nd Sikhs Infantry and the 5th Gurkha Rifles. He was appointed military attaché to the Foreign Office, Government of

India, and admitted to the Political Department in 1887. He then accompanied Sir Mortimer Durand on his missions to Sikkim in 1888, and again in 1893.

On 20 December 1891 at Nilt, Lieutenant Manners-Smith led a small party of men up a steep cliff in an attack on a strong enemy position, which had barred any advance for seventeen days. Avoiding rocks which were dropped from above, he was the first man to reach the summit. He then led his men in a charge against the enemy, shooting the first tribesman himself and taking the position.

His VC was gazetted on 12 July 1892 and presented to him later the same year. In 1896 he married Bertha Mabel, eldest daughter of Philip Arderne Latham. Between the years 1889-1919 he held political appointments in Kashmir, Bundelkhand, Baluchistan, Rajputana, Central India and Nepal. He served in the Tirah Expedition of 1897-98, following which he became political resident of the Political Department, Government of India and agent to the Governor General in Rajputana in 1917. After the First World War he retired to London.

Manners-Smith died from a wasting disease on 6 January 1920 and is buried in Kensal Green Cemetery, Square 187, Row 4, Grave 46720, London.

His VC is held by the Gurkha Museum, Peninsula Barracks, Winchester, Hampshire.

Second Gambia Campaign (1891-92)

In 1891 a party from the Anglo-French Boundary Commission was attacked by tribesmen led by Fodeh Cabbah, several of the group being wounded. Then HMS Alecto arrived, and a landing party was sent ashore. The situation was defused when a local chief, hearing of the expedition, came to meet them and apologised. The men returned to the ship, but Cabbah continued to cause trouble. A punitive expedition was sent to capture him.

William James GORDON
TONIATABA
13 March 1892

William Gordon was born on 19 May 1864 in Jamaica, West Indies. He enlisted into the West India Regiment in July 1885, before being posted with his regiment for a second tour of duty to West Africa in 1892.

On 13 March 1892, at Toniataba, Lance Corporal Gordon was one of a party of men under Major G. C. Madden attempting to break down the south gate of the town with a battering ram. Suddenly several musket barrels appeared through loopholes in the walls and were aimed at the major while his back was turned. Gordon called, 'Look out, sir!' and flung himself between the major and pushed him out of the way as the muskets fired. Gordon was shot through the lungs, but Madden was unhurt.

Gordon's VC was gazetted on 9 December 1892, and he was presented with it on 7 February 1893, while still in West Africa. His original VC was stolen in 1892, but an official replacement was issued the same year. Gordon retired from the army with a pension in April 1902, having reached the rank of sergeant.

He died from natural causes on 15 August 1922 and is buried in Kingston (Up Park Camp) Military Cemetery; Grave 244, Camp Road, Kingston, Jamaica.

His replacement VC is held by the Jamaican Military Museum, Kingston, Jamaica.

Kachin Hills Expedition (1892-93)

During the 1880s British and Indian troops were deployed throughout the operational zones of Burma to control the border 'dacoits', who rose up against the British presence in their region. By 1891, while the northern area of Burma held by the British was under control, the Kachin tribe continued plundering caravans and preying on travellers. In December 1885 a British force moved in to occupy the Bhamo region of the Kachin hills. They resisted annexation fiercely, and when they attacked a military police column an expedition was sent in to restore order.

<u>Owen Edward Pennefather LLOYD</u>
<u>FORT SIMA</u>
<u>6 January 1893</u>

Owen Edward Pennefather Lloyd VC

Lloyd was born on 1 January 1854 in County Roscommon, Ireland, the son of Major M. Pennefather Lloyd. He was educated at Fermoy College, Cork and Queen's University, Cork, and obtained three medical degrees at Edinburgh University. Lloyd enlisted into the Army Medical Service (later the Royal Army Medical Corps) in 1878 and served throughout the Anglo-Zulu War the following year, being present at the capture of Sekukuni's Stronghold. He also served in the First Boer War.

On 6 January 1893 at Fort Sima, Surgeon Major Lloyd and Subadar Matab Singh went to the assistance of the mortally wounded Captain Morton and treated his wounds while the enemy were only about 15 paces away and firing heavily. Matab Singh went back to fetch further help while Lloyd stayed with the wounded officer. Lloyd was wounded returning to the fort while carrying Morton.

Lloyd's VC was gazetted on 2 January 1894, and he was presented with it by Brigadier General George Bird in Mandalay, Burma, on 24 March 1894. He married Florence Morgan, and they had a son and a daughter. Lloyd became medical officer to the Franco-British Boundary Commission on the Burma Frontier, 1898-99. He then became the principal medical officer to the Bareilly Brigades in India and honourable surgeon to the Viceroy of India, following which he was appointed principal medical officer in South Africa. Lloyd retired in 1913 and enjoyed big game hunting, eventually settling on the south coast of England.

Lloyd died on 5 July 1941 and is buried in Kensal Green Cemetery; Square 188, Row 3, Grave 44252, Harrow Road, London.

His VC is held by the Museum of Military Medicine, Keogh Barracks, Aldershot, Surrey.

Chitral Expedition (1895)

In 1889 the British entered the Chitral district of India (now Pakistan) and established an agency, to which the local tribesmen were very hostile. In 1895 the Chitral chief was murdered. This signalled the start of fighting among local tribes. When Umrah Khan, ruler of the Narai district, invaded Chitral, Britain sent in four hundred men to restore order.

Harry Frederick WHITCHURCH
CHITRAL FORT
3 March 1895

Harry Frederick Whitchurch VC

Harry Whitchurch was born on 22 September 1866 in London, the son of Frederick Whitchurch. Educated in London, France and Germany, he entered a medical career in St. Bartholomew's Hospital, London in 1883. Whitchurch served in the 1892 Expedition to Lushai.

On 3 March 1895 Surgeon Captain Whitchurch was serving in the Indian Medical Service when, during a sortie from Fort Chitral, he went out to the assistance of Captain Baird (of the 24th Bengal Infantry) who was lying wounded one and a half miles from the fort. The wounded man was placed in a dhooli (a rudimentary litter or stretcher), but on the return journey three of the bearers were killed and the fourth wounded, so Whitchurch took the wounded man on his back and carried him for some distance. They were fired on incessantly the whole way, but he eventually succeeded in getting them back to the fort, although they were nearly all wounded and Baird died.

His VC was gazetted on 16 July 1895, and it was presented to him by Queen Victoria at Osborne House on 27 July 1895. During 1897-98 Whitchurch took part in the defence of Malakand and in the relief of Chakdara, as well as the engagement at Landakai on the North-West Frontier. In 1901 he was in China and took part in the relief of the Chinese Legation during the Boxer Rebellion, following which he was posted to India, where he served with the 1st Gurkha Rifles.

Whitchurch died from enteric fever on 16 August 1907 and is buried in Dharmsala Churchyard, India.

His VC is in The Ashcroft Gallery, Imperial War Museum, London

4

1896 - 1901

Matabeleland Rebellion (1896)

In 1895 all territories subject to the British South Africa Company were drawn together under the name of Rhodesia. By the end of March 1896 conditions for the Matabele tribesmen were so bad that they rose up in rebellion.

Herbert Stephen HENDERSON
BULAWAYO
30 March 1896

Herbert Stephen Henderson VC

Henderson was born on 30 March 1870 in Glasgow, the fourth son of William Henderson. He was educated at Kelvinside Academy, Hillhead, and served a five year apprenticeship at J & J Thomson Engineers, Glasgow, following which he moved to Belfast to work for

Workman, Clark & Co., and Harland & Wolff. In 1892 Henderson left Belfast to work in South Africa, and in 1894 moved to Rhodesia to work as an engineer in the Queen's Mine.

On 30 March 1896, at Bulawayo, Trooper Henderson, now serving in the Bulawayo Field Force, was on patrol in an advanced position when they were ambushed, and he and Trooper Celliers were cut off from the rest of the men. Celliers was shot in the knee and his horse was killed. Henderson put the wounded man on his own horse, and led him back 35 miles to Bulawayo, travelling by night and hiding during the day. A number of times Celliers asked Henderson to leave him, but he refused. They arrived three days later having had almost nothing to eat. Unfortunately Celliers died from his wounds two months later. Henderson later said, 'I never wish to spend another birthday like it!'

Henderson's VC was gazetted on 7 May 1897, and he was presented with it by the Governor of the Cape Colony, Lord Milner, in Bulawayo on 14 November 1897. After the rebellion was over he returned to mining, remaining in this profession for the rest of his life.

Henderson died from duodenal ulcer complications on 10 August 1942 and is buried in Bulawayo Town Cemetery (also known as Centenary Park Cemetery); General Section 2, Grave 887. Harare, Zimbabwe.

His VC is held by the National Army Museum, London.

Frank William BAXTER
UMGUZA RIVER
22 April 1896

Frank William Baxter VC

Frank Baxter was born on 29 December 1869 in London. As a young man he travelled to South Africa and in 1890 accompanied the Pioneer Column into Rhodesia (now Zimbabwe) but was discharged the following year. Baxter took up farming at Umtali and also had a number of interests in mining. He became a member of the Grey's Scouts, a local defence force. On the outbreak of the Matabeleland Rebellion Baxter enlisted into the Bulawayo Field Force.

On 22 April 1896, at the Umguza River, when during a retreat from a large enemy force, Trooper Baxter noticed that Trooper Wise had been wounded and dismounted. Baxter selflessly gave his horse to Trooper Wise, allowing Wise to gallop away to safety. As the enemy approached Baxter, three of his comrades rode past and tried to lift him to safety, but they all failed, and Baxter was killed moments later.

He is buried in Bulawayo Town Cemetery (also known as Centenary Park Cemetery); General Section 1, Grave 114. Harare, Zimbabwe.

On 7 May 1896 it was noted in the gazette that had he survived he would have been recommended for the VC, as it was not awarded posthumously at that time. His VC was gazetted on 15 January 1907 and posted to his father.

It is now in The Ashcroft Gallery, Imperial War Museum, London.

Mashona Rebellion (1896-97)

Anti-colonial feelings among the tribal people of Rhodesia had been running high for a long time but in June 1896, the Mashona tribe revolted, fired up by their spirit mediums who convinced them they would be impervious to bullets.

Randolph Cosby NESBITT
ALICE MINE MAZOE VALLEY
19 June 1896

Randolph Cosby Nesbitt VC

Randolph Nesbitt was born on 20 September 1867 in Queenstown, Cape Colony, South Africa, the son of Major C. A. Nesbitt. He was educated at St. Paul's School, London, but returned to South Africa in August 1885 to join the Cape Mounted Rifles. Nesbitt served throughout the Mashona Expedition of 1890 and was promoted to lieutenant in September 1891. He was Chief Constable at Fort Peddie, in the Cape, from March 1892 until April 1893 and at the end of that year he returned to Mashonaland to become an Inspector of Mounted Police. In 1894 he served in Gazaland on special service and the following year he was appointed a justice of the peace. In June 1895 Nesbitt was promoted to captain in the British South Africa Police.

On 19 June 1896, at the Alice Mine in the Mazoe Valley, Captain Nesbitt was serving in the Mashonaland Mounted Police when he led a patrol of only 13 men to the rescue of miners who were surrounded by hordes of rebels. Nesbitt and his men fought their way through the enemy and succeeded in getting the beleaguered miners and three women back to the nearby town of Salisbury, in spite of heavy fighting in which three of the small party were killed and five wounded.

Nesbitt's VC was gazetted on 7 May 1897, and he was presented with it by the Governor of the Cape Colony, Lord Milner, in Salisbury on 11 November 1897. He said he was always very embarrassed at having been singled out for the award; he felt the whole party had behaved heroically.

Nesbitt served in the Second Boer War as commanding officer of a squadron of the South Africa Police. In 1909 he became a Native Commissioner of the British South Africa Police. By the time of his retirement he had reached the rank of major.

He died on 23 July 1956, following a short illness, and his ashes are interred in The Cloisters, Anglican Cathedral, British South Africa Police Section, Harare, Zimbabwe.

His VC is held by the National Archives of Zimbabwe, Harare, Zimbabwe.

Malakand Frontier War (1897-98)

In 1894 the new frontier between India and Afghanistan was finalised by Colonel Sir Mortimer Durand's commission, bringing many tribes under Britain's influence. These tribes were extremely hostile to this annexation and widespread unrest followed. Then in 1897 the Amir of Afghanistan published a fiercely anti-Christian work in his assumed capacity as the King of Islam. This incited uprisings against the British garrisons all along the frontier.

Edmond William COSTELLO
MALAKAND
26 July 1897

Edmond William Costello VC

Edmond Costello was born on 7 August 1873 in Sheikhbudia, on the North-West Frontier of India, the son of Colonel C. P. Costello (of the Indian Medical Service) and Mrs Costello (née Harkan). He was educated at Beaumont College, Stonyhurst College and the Royal Military College, Sandhurst. In 1892 Costello was commissioned into the West Yorkshire Regiment, but transferred to the Indian Army in 1894, being posted to the 22nd Punjab Infantry.

On 26 July 1897, at Malakand, Lieutenant Costello went out from the hospital enclosure and with the help of two sepoys; he brought in a wounded lance havildar lying some 60 yards away on a football field. The field was overrun with enemy swordsmen and raked with fire from both sides.

His VC was gazetted on 9 November 1897, and he was presented with it by Queen Victoria on 2 December 1897 at Windsor Castle. In 1900 he was appointed adjutant of his regiment and promoted to captain in 1901. Costello worked as a recruiting officer until 1908 when he served in the Mohmand operation. He was promoted to major in 1910 and in 1913 entered the Indian Staff College at Quetta, graduating just prior to the start of the First World War.

In 1914 he rejoined his regiment as second-in-command and was posted to Mesopotamia as part of the 17th Indian Infantry Brigade, where he served throughout the war. Costello was promoted to brevet colonel in 1916 and he was awarded the Distinguished Service Order in 1917. In May 1918 he took command of the 12th Indian Infantry Brigade with the rank of lieutenant colonel. He was mentioned five times in despatches and was also awarded the French Croix de Guerre.

In 1919 he was (again) promoted to brevet colonel and made joint commander of the Indian contingent at the Peace March in London. Costello was promoted to colonel in March 1920, although he had held the acting rank of brigadier-general since 1918. He was appointed Commander of the Royal Victorian Order (CVO) in the 1920 New Year Honours. In March 1921 he was posted to Palestine as temporary commander of the Palestine Defence Force and remained there to command a brigade in 1922. Costello retired the following year and became director of military studies at the University of Cambridge.

He died on 7 June 1949 and is buried in St. Mark's Parish Churchyard, Hadlow Down, Sussex.

His VC is held by the National Army Museum, London.

Mohmand Campaign (1897-98)

On 8 August 1897 Mohmand tribesmen raided Shabkadar near Peshawar, but the means to crush this uprising were already in the region. Two divisions of Sir Bindon Blood's expedition had advanced from Malakand, and these men would be used to do the work.

James Morris Colquhoun COLVIN
MOHMAND VALLEY
16 - 17 September 1897

James Morris Colquhoun Colvin VC

James Colvin was born on 26 August 1870 in Bijnor, United Provinces, India, the son of James Colquhoun Colvin, of the Bengal Civil Service and Camilla Fanny Marie Morris. He was educated at Charterhouse, Surrey and at the Royal Military Academy, Woolwich. He was awarded the Pollock Gold Medal and Memoir as a cadet under officer for distinguished proficiency; the Regulation Sword for exemplary conduct; a travelling clock, aneroid barometer, thermometer and compass for maths and mechanics. Colvin joined the Royal Engineers in July 1889, and served in the Chitral Relief Force in 1895.

On 16-17 September 1897, in the Mohmand Valley, Lieutenant Colvin was in a party of volunteers (including Lieutenant Watson (page 145) and Corporal James Smith (page 147)) in a bayonet charge on the burning village of Bilot, to try to dislodge the enemy who were inflicting losses on British troops. After Watson was wounded in the hand, Colvin made two more attempts to take the village. He did not desist in his efforts until he was severely wounded and had to be carried back. Colvin then made a further two attempts on the village. Corporal Smith, although injured, assisted in removing the wounded to shelter. All three men were awarded the VC.

Colvin's VC was gazetted on 20 May 1898 (the same day as Watson) and he was presented with it by Queen Victoria at Windsor Castle on 19 July 1898. Colvin served in the Second Boer War as a special service officer, and on the staff with the rank of brevet major. In January 1904 he married Katherine Way, and they had three children.

In 1909 he passed out from the staff college in Camberley, and was a general staff officer at Quetta, 1911-15. Colvin was promoted to lieutenant colonel in 1917 and became commandant to the 3rd Sappers and miners in Kirkee, India. He retired from the army with the rank of colonel and lived in East Anglia.

Colvin died on 7 December 1945 and his ashes were scattered at Ipswich Crematorium; December Section, Old Garden of Rest, Cemetery Lane, Ipswich, Suffolk.

His VC is held by his family.

Thomas Colclough WATSON
MOHMAND VALLEY
16 - 17 September 1897

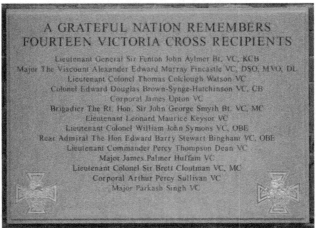

Thomas Colclough Watson VC

Thomas Watson was born on 11 April 1867 in Velsen, the Netherlands, the son of Thomas Colclough Watson and Eliza Holmes Reed. He was educated at Louth, Lincolnshire, and abroad. Watson entered the Royal Engineers in February 1888 and was posted to India, where he married Edythe Welchman in January 1892. Their only child, Gerald, was born in October 1892.

Edythe was awarded the Royal Red Cross (RRC) for her actions during the Black Mountains Expedition in 1888, making them, along with Lord Frederick Sleigh Roberts and Lady Roberts, the only two British officers and their wives to be awarded both the VC and the RRC.

On 16 - 17 September 1897, in the Mohmand Valley, Lieutenant Watson was in a party of volunteers (including Lieutenant Colvin (page 143) and Corporal James Smith (page 147)) in a bayonet charge on the burning village of Bilot, to try to dislodge the enemy who were inflicting losses on British troops. After being wounded in the hand, Colvin made two more attempts to take the village. He did not desist in his efforts until severely wounded and had to be carried back. Colvin then made a further two attempts on the village. Corporal Smith, although injured, assisted in removing the wounded to shelter. All three men were awarded the VC.

Watson's VC was gazetted on 20 May 1898 (the same day as Colvin) and he was presented with it by Queen Victoria at Windsor Castle on 23 June 1898. He remained in the Royal Engineers and served in Mesopotamia in 1915 with the rank of lieutenant colonel. In June of that year he was taken ill and invalided home.

Watson never fully recovered from his illness and died on 15 June 1917, his ashes are interred at Golders Green Crematorium; Niche 1153, East Columbarium, Hoop Lane, London.

His VC was sold at action in 2014 for £260,000 and is now in The Ashcroft Gallery, Imperial War Museum, London.

James SMITH
MOHMAND VALLEY
16 - 17 September 1897

James Smith VC

James Smith was born in 1871 in Maidstone, Kent. He enlisted into the East Kent Regiment (The Buffs) at an early age, was posted to India and promoted to corporal.

On 16-17 September 1897, in the Mohmand Valley, Corporal Smith was in a party of volunteers (with Lieutenants Colvin (page 143) and Watson (page 145)) in a bayonet charge on the burning village of Bilot. Although wounded himself, Smith assisted in removing the wounded to a place of safety. When Colvin left to get help, Smith was placed in charge. He held the position until his return, exposing himself to great danger and directing the fire of his men.

Smith was recommended for the VC by Watson, but it was not gazetted until 21 April 1899 and only after the matter was raised in Parliament. He was presented with his decoration by the General Officer Commanding Nagpur, Brigadier General Sir Richard Westmancott, on 5 July 1899. Smith continued to serve in India and retired with the rank of sergeant.

He died on 18 March 1946 and is buried in Watling Street Burial Ground: Section Daisy, Grave 4134, Dartford, Kent.

His VC is held by the National Army Museum, London.

Tirah Campaign (1897-98)

As a result of a series of individual uprisings by Afghans against the British, fighting broke out in the Tirah region. This was put down by Lockhart's punitive expedition.

Robert Bellew ADAMS
NAWA KILI
17 August 1897

Robert Bellew Adams VC

Robert Adams was born on 26 July 1856 in Muree, India, the son of Major Robert Roy Adams (of the Bengal Staff Corps) and Frances Charlotte Bellow. Sadly Major Adams was murdered by a fanatic in Peshawar in 1865, when his son was just nine years old. Young Robert was educated privately before attending the Forest School, Walthamstow, London.

Adams was commissioned a sub lieutenant in the 12th Regiment of Foot in September 1876 and served in India until 1879, when he was promoted to lieutenant. He transferred into the 3rd Punjab Cavalry and served with the Queen's Own Corps of Guides during the Afghan War of 1879-80. He marched with the Corps to Kabul and was present at all of the subsequent operations. Adams was appointed the officiating adjutant of the Corps in July 1880 and was mentioned in despatches. He was promoted to captain in 1887.

In 1895 Adams served with the Chitral Relief Force in command of the Guides Cavalry and, following the death in action of Lieutenant Colonel Battye, commanded the Corps of Guides Infantry. He was present at the storming of the Malakand Pass, the action near Khar, at the passage of the River Swat, and at Mamugai. Adams was mentioned in despatches twice and was given the brevet rank of lieutenant colonel with the substantive rank of major in September 1896.

On 17 August 1897, at Nawa Kili, while serving with the Malakand Force, Brevet Lieutenant Colonel Adams with the help of Lieutenant Alexander Fincastle, Lieutenant Hector MacLean and five guides went to the assistance of Lieutenant Greaves (correspondent for the *Times of India*) who had fallen wounded from his horse and had been set upon by the enemy with tulwars (swords) and knives. The enemy were driven away and Adams held them off while Fincastle and MacLean attempted to move Greaves, but he was shot and killed. MacLean was also mortally wounded during this action. Fincastle (page 150) and MacLean (page 151) were also awarded the VC for this action.

Adam's VC was gazetted on 9 November 1897 and was presented to him by Queen Victoria at Windsor Castle on 9 July 1898, following which, he returned to India and took part in the Buner Field Force, being mentioned in despatches. In April 1899 Adams was appointed commander of the Queen's Own Corps of Guides, and in September 1901 he was appointed aide-de-camp to King Edward VII.

Adams was promoted to major general in 1906, but an illness brought on by an accident in 1908 forced him to retire in 1911. Adams died on 13 February 1928 and his ashes are interned in Tomnahurich Cemetery, Inverness.

His VC is not publicly held.

His second cousin, Edward Bellew, was awarded the VC during the Second Battle of Ypres, in 1915.

Alexander Edward MURRAY
NAWA KILI
17 August 1897

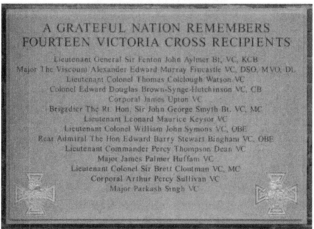

Alexander Edward Murray VC

Alexander Edward Murray, also known by the courtesy title of Viscount Fincastle, was born on 22 April 1871 in London, the son of Charles, 7th Duke of Dunmore, and Lady Gertrude Coke. Alexander immediately took the title of Viscount Fincastle. He was educated privately and at Eton, prior to joining the army in 1891, and was promoted to lieutenant in 1894.

Fincastle was posted to India and became aide-de-camp to the Viceroy of India between 1895 and 1897. He served in the Dongola Expedition in 1896, and the Malakand Frontier War, during which his horse was shot from under him.

On 17 August 1897, at Nawa Kili, Lieutenant Fincastle was serving in the Corps of Guides Cavalry when he, with Brevet Lieutenant Colonel Robert Adams, Lieutenant Hector MacLean and five guides went to the assistance of Lieutenant Greaves (correspondent for the *Times of India*) who had fallen wounded from his horse and had been set upon by the enemy with tulwars (swords) and knives. The enemy were driven away, and Adams held them off while Fincastle and MacLean attempted to move him, but he was shot and killed. MacLean was also mortally wounded during this action.

Fincastle's VC was gazetted on 9 November 1897 (the same day as Adams) and he was presented with it by Queen Victoria at Windsor Castle on 28 February 1898. He was promoted to captain in 1899 and served on the staff throughout the Second Boer War with the 6th (Inniskilling) Dragoons and 16th Lancers and was mentioned in despatches. He commanded the Imperial Yeomanry in the immediate aftermath of the war.

In January 1904 he married Lucinda Dorothea Kemble, and they had one son and two daughters. He succeeded his father as the 8th Earl of Dunmore in 1907 and, as Lord Dunmore, served in the First World War, was wounded, awarded the Distinguished Service Order and mentioned in despatches four times. After the war he commanded the 16th Lancers with the rank of lieutenant colonel.

Fincastle died on 29 January 1962 and was cremated under the name Murray. His ashes were scattered at Golders Green Crematorium; Section 4-C, Garden of Remembrance, Hoop Lane, London.

His VC is not publicly held.

Hector Lachlan Stewart MacLEAN
NAWA KILI
17 August 1897

Hector Lachlan Stewart MacLean VC

Hector MacLean was born on 13 September 1870 in Bunna, on the North-West Frontier of India (now Pakistan), the oldest son of Major General Charles Smith MacLean and Margaret MacQueen Bairnsfather. He was educated at St. Salvador's School and Fettes College, Edinburgh, before joining the Northumberland Fusiliers as a second lieutenant in April 1889.

Posted to India, MacLean became Probationer for the Indian Staff Corps in 1891, and in March joined the Corps of Guides. He took part in the Hazara Expedition of 1891 and the Chitral Expedition of 1895 and was appointed adjutant to the Corps of Guides in 1896.

On 17 August 1897, at Nawa Kili, Lieutenant Maclean, with Brevet Lieutenant Colonel Robert Adams, Lieutenant Alexander Fincastle and five guides went to the assistance of Lieutenant Greaves (correspondent for the *Times of India*) who had fallen from his pony and was set upon by the enemy with tulwars (swords) and knives. The enemy were driven away, and Adams held them off while Fincastle and MacLean attempted to move him, but he was shot and killed.

MacLean was also mortally wounded during this action and is buried in the Guides Cemetery, St Alban's Churchyard, Mardan, now in Pakistan. He was recommended for the VC, but it was not awarded posthumously at that time (although there was nothing in the Royal Warrant to this effect, but it had been practice not to do so). Once a change of policy came into effect (after the posthumous award to Lord Roberts in 1900) MacLean's VC was gazetted on 15 January 1907, along with a number of other backdated awards.

His VC is in The Ashcroft Gallery, Imperial War Museum, London.

Henry Singleton PENNELL
DARGAI HEIGHTS
20 October 1897

Henry Singleton Pennell VC

Henry Pennell was born on 18 June 1874 in Dawlish, Devon, the second son of Edwin Francis Pennell and Henrietta Copeland. He was educated locally and at 13 was sent to Eastbourne College, following which he was accepted by the Royal Military College, Sandhurst. On passing out in October 1893 Pennell was commissioned a second lieutenant in the 2nd Battalion, the Derbyshire Regiment (the Sherwood Foresters). He was promoted to lieutenant in 1896 before being posted overseas on Christmas Eve the same year.

On 20 October 1897, at the Dargai Heights, during the attack Captain W. Smith was wounded and lying in the open. Lieutenant Pennell ran to his assistance and under heavy fire tried twice to bring in the wounded man, only giving up when he realised Smith had died.

Pennell's VC was gazetted on 20 May 1898, and he was presented with it by Colonel Dowse at Bareilly, India on 2 September 1898.

He took part in the affair at Dargai, was present at the Sampagha Pass, the Arhanga Pass, and the operations in Kanki, Warren and Bazar Valley. In 1899 he was attached to the West Yorkshire Regiment, with whom he saw service in the Second Boer War. Pennell saw action at all the major actions in the attempts to relieve Ladysmith, including Colenso, Spion Kop, Vaal Krantz and the Tugela, which saw the capture of Pieter's Hill, which left Pennell severely wounded. He was mentioned in despatches twice.

In 1905 Pennell was appointed staff-captain at the Administrative Headquarters, Southern Command. In January 1907 he and fellow officers holidayed in St. Moritz, Switzerland and on 19 January they decided to take on the Cresta Run. The rider who preceded Pennell had fallen at the corner known as Battledore and spectators had rushed forward to assist the fallen man. In doing so they trampled down the deep snow which protected fallen riders. Pennell, following at speeds of 40/50mph, fell at the same corner but now, with no snow to protect him, he hit the rocks, suffering severe internal injuries from which he died.

Pennell's body was brought home, and he is buried in St. Gregory's Churchyard, Dawlish, Devon.

His VC is held by the Museum of the Mercian Regiment, The Castle, Nottingham.

George Frederick FINDLATER
DARGAI HEIGHTS
20 October 1897

George Frederick Findlater VC

George Findlater was born on 16 February 1872 in Turriff, Aberdeenshire, Scotland, one of eleven children of Alexander Findlater and Mary Ann Clark. He was educated at school in Turriff but at thirteen left to work as a farm labourer. Three years later he enlisted into the 2nd Battalion, the Gordon Highlanders, and was posted to Ceylon with his battalion. In 1891 he transferred to the 1st Battalion, then serving on the North-West Frontier of India. Findlater first saw action at the Malakand Pass in March 1895 where he was hit but not actually wounded. Later the same year he served with the relief force in the Chitral Expedition. In 1896 Findlater was appointed a piper with his battalion.

On 20 October 1897, at the Dargai Heights, during the attack, Piper Findlater was hit in the foot, but carried on. He was then hit in the ankle and finding he could not stand, propped himself up against a boulder and went on playing the pipes under heavy fire to encourage the advance. Officially it is said he played 'Cock o'the North' but he later said that he played 'Haughs of Cromdale.'

His VC was gazetted on 20 May 1898, although he had been presented with it six days previously (the same day as Samuel Vickery (page 157)) by Queen Victoria while he was convalescing from his wounds at the Netley Hospital in Southampton. He was offered a position, probably at Balmoral, which he turned down due to the low pay. Finding that he had become something of a celebrity, Findlater soon found he could earn good money by appearing in music halls, re-enacting his actions nightly on stage, much to the disapproval of the War Office. In 1899 he married his cousin, Nellie Findlater, and they had four children. Findlater took up farming until 1914 when he volunteered for service at 42 years of age. In 1915, now a sergeant piper, he was wounded at Loos and was invalided out of the army. On his return home he took up farming again.

Findlater died from a heart attack on 4 March 1942 and is buried in Forglen Cemetery, near Turriff, Scotland.

His VC is held by the Gordon Highlanders Museum, Aberdeen.

Edward LAWSON
DARGAI HEIGHTS
20 October 1897

Edward Lawson VC

Edward Lawson was born on 11 April 1873 in Newcastle-upon-Tyne. He enlisted into the 1st Battalion, the Gordon Highlanders, around 1893 and was posted to India's North-West Frontier with his regiment.

On 20 October 1897, at the Dargai Heights, during the attack, Lieutenant K. Dingwall was wounded. Private Lawson rushed to his aid under heavy fire and carried him out of danger, and then went back to pick up Private MacMillan and bring him to safety. This, despite being wounded twice himself.

His VC was gazetted on 20 May 1898, and he was presented with it by Queen Victoria on 25 June 1898, most likely at Windsor Castle.

He was discharged from the army in 1902. Following this he served as a sergeant with the Northern Cyclist Battalion before and during the First World War.

Lawson died on 2 July 1955 and is buried in Heaton Cemetery; Section 2, Grave 56, Benton Road, Newcastle-upon-Tyne, Tyne & Wear.

His VC is held by the Gordon Highlanders Museum, Aberdeen.

Samuel VICKERY
DARGAI HEIGHTS, 20 October 1897
& WARAN VALLEY, 16 November 1897

Samuel Vickery VC

Samuel Vickery was born on 6 February 1873 in Wambrook, Somerset. At the age of 20 he enlisted into the army and completed his training at the Dorset Regiment's depot barracks in what was by now his hometown of Dorchester. After a period of service with the 2nd Battalion, Vickery was part of a draft sent to India to bring the 1st Battalion of the Dorset Regiment up to operational strength.

On 20 October 1897, at the Dargai Heights, Private Vickery ran down the slope and rescued a wounded man under heavy fire, bringing him back to cover. On 16th November, in the Waran Valley, he distinguished himself again, killing three of the enemy who attacked him when he was separated from his company. He was later sent home suffering from a chipped bone in his foot.

Vickery's VC was gazetted on 20 May 1898, although he had been presented with it six days previously (the same day as Frederick Findlater (page 154)) by Queen Victoria while he was convalescing from his wounds at the Netley Hospital in Southampton.

Six years later Corporal Vickery was serving in the Boer War having been attached to the 2nd Mounted Infantry. He was captured by the Boers, but just four days later made a daring escape and rejoined his unit. He was subsequently wounded at Nooitgedacht during the guerrilla war.

Vickery retired from the army with the rank of sergeant but, upon the outbreak of the First World War he re-enlisted into the 1st Battalion, the Dorsetshire Regiment, seeing heavy fighting in the Ypres Salient.

Vickery died on 20 June 1952 and his ashes were scattered at Glyntaff Crematorium; Lawn 4, Plot 4, Cemetery Road, Pontypridd, Mid-Glamorgan.

His VC is held by the Devonshire and Dorset Regimental Museum, The Keep, Dorchester, Dorset.

Second Sudan Campaign (1896-1900)

The defeat of General Gordon in 1885 was seen as a major British humiliation, but nothing was done until Lord Salisbury came to power in 1895. By then the government was concerned with the Khalifa's regime in Sudan, which bordered the British held Egypt. In March 1896 the Egyptian army under Kitchener was ordered in the Sudan.

Paul Aloysius KENNA
OMDURMAN
2 September 1898

BRIGADIER GENERAL
P. A. KENNA
VC., DSO., ADC.
21ST (E OF I LANCERS)
COMDG. 3RD MOUNTED BRIG.
30TH AUGUST 1915 AGE 53

ON WHOSE SOUL
SWEET JESUS HAVE MERCY
MAY HE REST IN PEACE

Paul Aloysius Kenna VC

Paul Kenna was born on 16 August 1862 in Liverpool, the son of Thomas Kenna, a wealthy stockbroker. Kenna was educated at Stonyhurst College and St. Francis Xavier College, Liverpool. On passing out of the Royal Military College, Sandhurst he was commissioned into the 2nd West India Regiment, serving with them for two years in the West Indies and West Africa. In 1895 he saved the life of a drowning man and was awarded the Royal Humane Society Certificate. In the same year he married Lady Cecil Bertie but sadly she died, and Kenna married again to Angela Mary, and they had two daughters. In 1889 Kenna transferred to the 21st Hussars, which in 1897 became the 21st Lancers (Empress of India's).

On 2 September 1898, at Omdurman, during the charge of the 21st Lancers, upon seeing that Major Crole Wyndham's horse had been killed, Captain Kenna rode up to and took him onto his own horse and rode away to safety. He then, together with Corporal Swarbrick, rode to the assistance of Lieutenant de Montmorency (page 160) who was dismounted amidst the enemy and was trying to help Lieutenant R. Grenfell. Kenna kept the enemy off with his revolver while Swarbrick caught the lieutenant's horse which had previously bolted. They were then able to return to their regiment.

Kenna's VC was gazetted on 15 November 1898, and he was presented with it by Queen Victoria at Osborne House on 6 January 1899.

He was soon back in action, this time in the Boer War of 1899-1902, first as assistant provost marshal on General French's Staff, then he was appointed brigade major in 1900. In 1901 he was given command of a column with the rank of brevet major. Kenna took part in the relief of Kimberley, in the Orange Free State, and later served in the Transvaal. He also served on the Zululand Frontier, being mentioned in despatches twice and awarded the Distinguished Service Order.

Kenna was promoted to substantive major in September 1902 and shortly after was selected for special service with the Somaliland Field Force commanding the Mounted Troops throughout the campaign, being mentioned in despatches three times.

In 1904 he was promoted to brevet lieutenant colonel. At the conclusion of the campaign Kenna returned to duty with his regiment in England. Appointed brigade major to the 1st Cavalry Brigade in October 1905, he held that position until September 1906 when he was given command of the 21st Lancers. He was promoted to brevet colonel in December of the same year and appointed aide-de-camp to King Edward VII.

In September 1910 he was promoted to colonel and in April 1911 took over command of the Nottinghamshire and Derbyshire Mounted Rifles.

He was a member of the 1912 Olympics team with Brian Lawrence VC, and in 1913 he won the King's Cup for riding. Kenna was promoted to brigadier general in August 1914 and in the spring of 1915 took his brigade to Egypt, and from there to Gallipoli.

On 30 August 1915, while making a tour of inspection of the front line, Kenna was severely wounded by a sniper and died later that day. He is buried in Lala Baba Cemetery; Plot II, Row A, Grave 1, Gallipoli, Turkey.

His VC is held by the Royal Lancers & Nottinghamshire Yeomanry Museum, Thoresby Park, Nottinghamshire.

Raymond Harvey Lodge Joseph de MONTMORENCY
OMDURMAN
2 September 1898

Raymond Harvey Lodge Joseph de Montmorency VC

Raymond de Montmorency was born on 5 February 1867 in Montreal, Quebec, Canada, the eldest son of Major General Reymond de Montmorency, 3rd Viscount Frankfort de Montmorency. He was commissioned a second lieutenant in September 1887 and joined the 21st Lancers (Empress of India's). De Montmorency was promoted to lieutenant in 1889 and became adjutant in 1893.

On 2 September 1898, at Omdurman, after the charge of the 21st Lancers, Lieutenant de Montmorency went to the assistance of Lieutenant R. Grenfell who was lying surrounded by a great many Dervishes. He drove off the enemy and, finding that the lieutenant was dead, put Grenfell's body on his horse which then bolted. Captain Paul Kenna and Corporal Swarbrick then came to his assistance and together they were able to return to their regiment.

De Montmorency's VC was gazetted on 15 November 1898, and he was presented with it by Queen Victoria at Osborne House on 6 January 1899. Shortly afterwards he was posted to South Africa for service in the Boer War with the rank of captain.

On 23 February 1900, near Stormberg, de Montmorency was leading a reconnaissance party when he was mortally wounded. He kept up fire on the enemy position in order to allow the remaining men to retire. He is buried in Molteno Cemetery, near Dordrecht, South Africa.

His VC is not publicly held.

Thomas **BYRNE**
OMDURMAN
2 September 1898

Thomas Byrne VC

Thomas 'Paddy' Byrne was born in December 1866 in Dublin, Ireland. Byrne enlisted into the 8th Hussars at the age of 20 and served with them for over a year, before he transferred to the 21st Lancers (Empress of India's). He would serve for over 22 years with the regiment overseas, the first eight in India, then two in Egypt, and then for one year in South Africa, following which he was posted to Sudan.

On 2 September 1898, at Omdurman, during the charge of the 21st Lancers, Private Byrne, despite having been wounded in the right arm, went to the assistance of Lieutenant Molyneux who was wounded, unhorsed and surrounded by Dervishes. Byrne attacked these men, receiving a severe wound to the chest, but his gallant action enabled the lieutenant to escape. It was Winston Churchill (then correspondent for the *Morning Post*), who rode in the charge and identified Byrne as Molyneux's saviour. Churchill later said, 'It was the bravest act I had ever seen performed.'

His VC was gazetted on 15 November 1899, and he was presented it by Queen Victoria at Osborne House on 6 January 1899, while still recovering from his wounds. After his service was over he settled in Kent.

Byrne died on 17 February 1944 and is buried in Canterbury City Cemetery; RC Section MJ, Grave 22, Westgate Court Avenue, Canterbury, Kent.

His original VC was stolen from his son Edward, while he was serving in East Africa in 1949. Edward kept the VC pinned to the inside of his jacket, and while working as a military policeman the jacket was stolen. The decoration has never been seen publicly again. In 1976 Thomas' grandson applied for and was granted an official replacement VC, but in 1978 this decoration was sold at auction for £700. Upon hearing the news, Queen Elizabeth II stated that she would never again approve an official replacement VC. The decoration was put up for sale again in 1979 but went unsold. In 1996 the VC was again sold at auction for £6,500. The last that was heard of it was in 2015, when it was sold at auction for £40,000 to an unknown buyer.

Nevill Maskelyne SMYTH
OMDURMAN
2 September 1898

Nevill Maskelyne Smyth VC

Nevill Smyth was born on 14 August 1868 in London, the second son of Sir Warington Wilkinson Smyth, a noted geologist. He was educated at Westminster School and at the Royal Military College, Sandhurst. Upon his graduation in 1888 he was posted to the 2nd Dragoon Guards (Queen's Bays) and reported to them in India with the rank of second lieutenant.

In 1890 Smyth was attached to the Royal Engineers to assist with a railway survey during the Zhob Valley Expedition. During the Dongola Expedition of 1896, Smyth was employed on special service with the Intelligence Department. He was orderly officer to the Officer Commanding the Mounted Forces at the Battle of Firket and the pursuit to Suarda; was on the staff passing the flotilla up the Cataracts and acted as orderly officer to the Chief-of-Staff in the action at Hafir and the occupation of Dongola. He rode through the Dervishes with a message to the flotilla at Debba, for which he was mentioned in despatches.

During the Sudan Campaign Smyth was staff officer to Sir Leslie Rundle and was given command of the advanced post during the gunboat bombardment of Metemmeh and at the Battle of Atbara. On 2nd September 1898, at Omdurman, towards the end of the battle, Captain Smyth galloped forward and attacked an Arab who had run amok among some camp followers. Smyth killed the Arab, being wounded in the arm while doing so, saving the life of at least one war correspondent.

Smyth's VC was gazetted on 15 November 1898, and he was presented with it by Queen Victoria at Osborne House on 6 January 1899, following which he returned to Sudan to help suppress the uprising on the Blue Nile at Khalifa Sherif.

Smyth took part in the Second Boer War as a brevet major and he was promoted to major in 1903.

In 1912 he was promoted to colonel and from 1913-14 he was commandant of the Khartoum District. In 1915 Brigadier-General Smyth commanded the 1st Australian Infantry Brigade and saw action at Gallipoli. In 1916 he was present at the Battle of the Somme and the capture on the Hindenburg Line at Bullecourt and then the Third Battle of Ypres in 1917. He was mentioned in despatches eight times.

Smyth commanded the 58th London Division (1918) and the 59th Division (1918-19). Following his army career he retired and moved to Australia.

Smyth died on 21 July 1941 and is buried in Balmoral Cemetery, Victoria, Australia.

His VC is held by his family.

Alexander Gore Arkwright HORE-RUTHVEN
GEDARIF
22 September 1898

Alexander Gore Arkwright Hore-Ruthven VC

Alexander Hore-Ruthven was born on 6 July 1872 in Windsor, Berkshire, the son of the 8th Baron Ruthven and Lady Caroline Annesley-Gore. He was educated at Winchester College from 1884-85 and then Eton which, due to his poor eyesight, he left in 1888 and was sent into business by his parents.

Hore-Ruthven first worked in a tea merchant's office in Glasgow and later travelled to India to work on a tea plantation in Assam. However, he contracted malaria and returned to England in 1892. In May 1899 he joined the army and served as a captain in the 3rd (Militia) Battalion, the Highland Light Infantry, attached to the Egyptian Army in the Sudan Campaign.

On 22 September 1898, at Gedarif, Captain Hore-Ruthven saw an Egyptian officer lying wounded within 50 yards of the Dervishes, who were firing as they advanced. He picked up the wounded man and carried him to safety, but he had to put him down several times in order to fire upon the enemy to check their advance. Hore-Ruthven was mentioned in despatches three times for this campaign.

His VC was gazetted on 28 February 1899, and he was presented with it by Queen Victoria at Windsor Castle on 11 May 1899.

In December 1900 he was gazetted a lieutenant in the Cameron Highlanders, and from 1903-04 Hore-Ruthven was a special service officer in Somaliland. From 1905-08 he was military secretary and aide-de-camp to the Viceroy of Ireland, Lord Dudley. Hore-Ruthven was promoted to captain in the 1st Dragoons in April 1908 and in June the same year he married Zara Pollock, and they had two sons, one of whom died in infancy. Less than a year after his marriage he followed Lord Dudley as his military secretary to Australia, when the former was appointed governor general, a post he held until 1910.

Hore-Ruthven returned to military service in India when he was promoted to brigade major, and then major in the Welsh Guards in November 1914. During the First World War he served in France and Gallipoli, where he was severely wounded. He was mentioned in despatches five times and awarded the Distinguished Service Order & Bar and ended the war with the rank of brigadier general.

After the war he held various army staff positions until 1918 when he was appointed Governor of South Australia. In 1938 Hore-Ruthven was appointed Governor General of Australia. In 1945 he retired from public life and returned to England.

Hore-Ruthven died on 2 May 1955 and is buried (under the name Gore-Arkwright) in St. John the Baptist Churchyard, Church Lane, Shipton Moyne, near Malmesbury, Gloucestershire.

His VC is in The Ashcroft Gallery, Imperial War Museum, London.

Cretan Revolt (1897-98)

For many years the Turkish Muslim regime had oppressed the Christian people of Crete. In 1897, with the support of the Greek military, the Christians rose up in revolt. Britain, France, Russia, Italy, Germany and Austria sent warships to restore peace. However, no lasting solution was reached. By 1898 the British Garrison in Candia had been reduced to a single regiment. When, in September, the colonel attempted to install a new collector of tax, a Muslim mob protested and killed nearly a hundred British soldiers and a thousand Christian civilians. British ships bombarded the town and sent two parties of 50 men ashore to restore order.

William Job MAILLARD
CANDIA
6 September 1898

William Job Maillard VC

William Maillard was born on 10 March 1863 in Banwell, Somerset, the son of a Wesleyan minister and supposedly a descendant of Sir Francis Drake. The family name is said to be a corruption of Mallard, the French word for drake. He was educated at Kingswood School in Bath, Dunheved College, Cornwell and at Guy's Hospital, London, 1882-89. Upon qualifying in August 1889 he entered the Royal Navy as a surgeon.

On 6 September 1898, at Candia, Crete, his party was attacked while being brought ashore from HMS *Hazard*. Although he had already reached cover, he ran back to a boat to help Seaman Arthur Stroud, who was wounded. He tried to lift him but could not as the boat was drifting. When he returned to his post his clothes were found to be riddled with bullet holes.

Maillard's VC was gazetted on 2 December 1898, and he was presented with it by Queen Victoria at Buckingham Palace 13 days later.

He retired from the Royal Navy due to ill-health in 1902 and died on 10 September 1903.

Maillard is buried in Wimborne Road Cemetery; Plot 4 South, Row V, Grave 133, Wimborne Road, Lansdowne, Bournemouth, Dorset.

His VC is in The Ashcroft Gallery, Imperial War Museum, London. He remains the only naval medical officer to be awarded the VC and one of the few to be awarded for action when the country was not at war.

Boxer Rebellion (1899-1901)

In the late 1800s a society was formed, called the 'Boxers' by the west. Its objective was to rid China of foreigners and Christians. With the appointment of one of its founder members, Yu Hsien, as Governor of Shantung Province in March 1899, the way was clear for them to start their campaign. This is, interestingly, the only time both the VC and the USA's Medal of Honor were awarded for the same action.

<u>Lewis Stratford Tollemache HALLIDAY</u>
<u>PEKING</u>
<u>24 June 1900</u>

Lewis Stratford Tollemache Halliday VC

Lewis Halliday was born on 14 May 1870 in Medstead, Hampshire, the eldest son of Lieutenant Colonel Stratford C. Halliday of the Royal Artillery. He was educated at Elizabeth College, Guernsey, and entered the Royal Marine Light Infantry (RMLI) in September 1889. Halliday was promoted to captain in 1898. In May 1900 he disembarked from

HMS *Orlando* at Taku, China, in command of 50 men and marched to Peking, as Legation Guard.

On 24 June 1900, at Peking, during an attack on the British Legation, the Boxers set fire to the stables and occupied some adjoining buildings. It being imperative to drive them out, a hole was made in the legation wall and 20 men of the RMLI were sent in. Captain Halliday, leading a party of six men, was involved in desperate fighting and was severely wounded, but despite his injuries, he killed four of the enemy. Finally, unable to carry on, he ordered his men to go on without him. He then walked 3 miles unaided to the hospital although shot through his shoulder and having a punctured lung.

For his distinguished service in the field Halliday was promoted to brevet major in September 1900.

His VC was gazetted on 1 January 1901, and he was presented with it by Edward VII at St. James' Palace on 25 July 1901.

In 1904 he was given command of a unit from his corps onboard HMS *Empress of India*. In 1908 Halliday married Florence Clara Budgen and they had one son. From 1908 to 1911 he was commander of a company of Gentlemen Cadets at the Royal Military College, Sandhurst. In 1912 Halliday was appointed to serve on the staff of the Royal Naval War College, and also on the Royal Naval War Staff. Following the death of his first wife, Halliday married Violet Blake in 1916.

Halliday was one of 74 VC recipients to form the honour guard at the internment of the Unknown Warrior at Westminster Abbey on 11 November 1920.

He died on 9 March 1966 and his ashes are interned in Medstead Cemetery: Family Grave, South Town Road, Medstead, Hampshire.

His VC is held by the Royal Marines Museum, Southsea, Portsmouth, Hampshire.

Basil John Douglas GUY
TIENTSIN
13 July 1900

Basil John Douglas Guy VC

Basil Guy was born on 8 May 1882 in Bishop Auckland, County Durham, the son of the Reverend Sherwood Guy, Vicar of Christchurch, Harrogate. He was educated at Aysgarth School, Yorkshire, and Llandaff Cathedral School, before entering the Royal Navy Cadet ship HMS *Britannia*, moored at Dartmouth. In July 1898 Guy passed out of training as a midshipman and was posted to the pre-dreadnought HMS *Barfleur*, soon to be despatched to China.

On 13 July 1900 at Tientsin, during the advance of the Naval Brigade, Able Seaman McCarthy was wounded 50 yards from cover. Midshipman Guy went to his assistance but could not lift him. While Guy treated his wounds the enemy concentrated all their fire on them. By now the remainder of the force had forged ahead, finding cover. Guy ran to fetch some stretcher bearers; he placed the wounded man onto a stretcher. However, McCarthy was hit again and killed before he could be carried to safety.

Guy's VC was gazetted on 1 January 1901, and he was presented with it by Edward VII at Keyham Barracks, Devonport on 8 March 1902, and was promoted to lieutenant in July 1903.

During the First World War Lieutenant Commander Guy was skipper of the Q-ship (an armed merchant ship with concealed weapons designed to lure enemy submarines to the surface) HMS *Wonganella* and, for his actions against an enemy U-boat (submarine) in March 1917, he was awarded the Distinguished Service Order. In August 1917 he married Elizabeth Mary Arnold and in June 1918 he was promoted to commander. After serving for another five years he retired but was recalled for service during the Second World War, serving in staff appointments.

He died on 28 December 1956 and is buried in St. Michael's & All Angels Churchyard; Family Grave, Pirbright, Surrey.

His VC is in The Ashcroft Gallery, Imperial War Museum, London.

His brother Oswald was awarded the DSO, Military Cross and Bar during the First World War.

Third Ashanti Expedition (1900)

Being first suppressed in 1874, the Ashanti people of Gambia had risen again in 1895. This was crushed and a resentful peace followed until 1900, when the British decided to capture the symbolic 'Golden Stool' (the royal and divine throne of kings of the Ashanti people) regarded by the Ashanti as a sign of authority.

John Henry MACKENZIE
DOMPOASSI
6 June 1900

John Henry MacKenzie VC

John MacKenzie was born on 22 November 1871 in Contin, Ross-shire, Scotland. He enlisted in August 1887, at Fort George, Inverness. In December 1887 he was posted to the 1st Battalion, the Seaforth Highlanders, and was promoted to corporal in 1891, but on transferring to the 2nd Battalion he gave up his rank.

MacKenzie took part in the Relief of Chitral in 1895 and in 1897 was again promoted to corporal and awarded the Distinguished Conduct Medal. In November of that year he was posted to the Lagos Regiment on the West Coast of Africa and in March 1899 was promoted to sergeant. While in West Africa MacKenzie took part in three campaigns, being mentioned in despatches in each of them.

On 6 June 1900, at Dompoassi, Sergeant MacKenzie was wounded while working two Maxim guns under heavy fire. He nevertheless volunteered to clear the enemy from a strongly held stockade. His own company was ordered up and he led them into the charge. The enemy fled into the bush in confusion.

MacKenzie was given a commission of second lieutenant in November 1900.

His VC was gazetted on 15 January 1901, and he was presented with it by Edward VII at St. James' Palace on 12 April 1901.

In January 1904 he was promoted to captain in the Royal Scots; during this time he also served with the Northern Nigeria Regiment and was mentioned in despatches for his work in the Aro Expedition. He served on the staff of the Munster Field Force and during the Kano-Sokoto Expedition, being mentioned in despatches for both.

MacKenzie was promoted to major and was commanding officer of the 2nd Battalion, the Bedfordshire Regiment.

He was killed in action at Loos on 17 May 1915 and is buried in the Guards Cemetery: Plot VIII, Row J, Grave 10, Windy Corner, near Cuinchy, France.

His VC is held by the Queen's Own Highlanders Museum, Fort George, Ardersier, Inverness-shire, Scotland.

Charles John MELLISS
OBASSA
30 September 1900

Charles John Melliss VC

Charles Melliss was born on 12 September 1862 in Mhow, India, the son of Lieutenant General George Julius Melliss of the Indian Staff Corps. He was educated at Wellington College and the Royal Military College, Sandhurst, before joining the East Yorkshire Regiment in 1882, and was posted to India where he joined the Indian Staff Corps in 1884. Melliss served in East Africa against the Mazrui tribesmen in 1896.

In 1897-98 he served on the North-West Frontier, being present during the operations in the Kurram Valley in August and September 1897. Melliss also served in the Tirah Campaign of 1897-98, taking part in the action at Dargai and in the operations in the Bara Valley. Promoted to captain he served with the Northern Nigeria Regiment with the West African Frontier Force from 1898-1902.

On 30 September 1900, at Obassa, Captain Melliss collected as many men as he could and led a charge through the bush. Although wounded, he fought hand-to-hand during which he grappled with one of the enemy, before running him through with his sword. His bold rush caused panic among the enemy who were pursued by the Sikhs as they fled.

His VC was gazetted on 15 January 1901, and he was presented with it by Edward VII at St. James' Palace on 12 October 1901.

Earlier that year he was married to Kathleen Walter. From 1902-04 Melliss served in East Africa, taking part in operations in Somaliland, and was mentioned in despatches. At some time in 1903 he was attacked by a lion while hunting, almost losing an arm. From 1906-10 he commanded the 53rd Sikh Frontier Force and from 1907-12 was aide-de-camp to Edward VII.

In 1914 Melliss was attached to the 6th (Poona) Division as it moved into the Ottoman province of Basra. In April 1915 he was instrumental in the victory at Shaiba. Melliss fought at Ctesiphon, the furthest his division would advance. After Ctesiphon, General Townsend ordered a retreat, pursued by the Ottomans until they reached Kut-al-Amara, where the 6th was ordered to dig in and await relief. Melliss fell ill during the siege and was still in hospital when Townsend surrendered on 29 April 1916.

Transported upriver by steamship, Melliss remained in hospital and was unable to travel as the survivors were marched north towards Anatolia. When Melliss was well enough to follow he was allowed an escort and better supplies because he was a senior officer. Along the way they encountered sick and dying men. Melliss took any survivors he found with him; at each stop he insisted that these men, both British and Indian, be put into hospital.

Melliss spent two and a half years in Turkish prisons. For his services during the war he was mentioned in dispatches five times and was knighted in 1915. After his release, he returned to England and rose to the rank of major general before his retirement.

Melliss died on 6 June 1936 and is buried in St. Peter's Churchyard, Frimley Green Road, Frimley, Surrey.

His VC is held by Wellington College, Crowthorne, Berkshire.

APPENDIX – ALPAHBETICAL LIST

Each entry starts with the recipient's surname, in CAPITALS, their first name(s) and the page number in the text.

ADAMS, James William   87
ADAMS, Robert Bellew   148
ASHFORD, Thomas Elsdon   99
AYLMER, Fenton John   127

BAXTER, Frank William   138
BELL, David   53
BELL, Mark Sever   68
BERGIN, James   59
BOISRAGON, Guy Hudleston   129
BOYES, Duncan Gordon   41
BROWN, Peter   104
BURSLEM, Nathaniel Godolphin   12
BYRNE, Thomas   162

CHANNER, George Nicolas   70
CHAPLIN, John Worthy   19
CHASE, William St. Lucien   98
COLLIS, James   96
COLVIN, James Morris Colquhoun   143
COOK, John   74
COOPER, James   54
CORBETT, Frederick   111
COSTELLO, Edmond William   141
CREAGH, Garrett O'Moore   81
CRIMMIN, John   122

DE MONTMORENCY, Raymond H. L. J.   161
DICK-CUNYNGHAM, William Henry   89
DOUGLAS, Campbell Mellis   52
DOWN, John Thornton   26
DUNDAS, James   47

EDWARDS, Thomas   119
EDWARDS, William Mordaunt Marsh   113
EMBLETON, David   111

FINDLATER, George Frederick   155
FITZGIBBON, Andrew   20
FITZPATRICK, Francis   106
FLAWN, Thomas   107
FOSBERY, George Vincent   22

GIFFORD, Edric Frederick   63
GORDON, William James   132
GRANT, Charles James William   125
GRIFFITHS, William   55
GUY, Basil John Douglas   170

HALLIDAY, Lewis Stratford Tollemache   168
HAMILTON, Walter Richard Pollock   79
HAMMOND, Arthur George   90
HARDING, Israel   110
HART, Reginald Clare   76
HARTLEY, Edmund Barron   105
HEAPHY, Charles   31
HENDERSON, Herbert Stephen   136
HINCKLEY, George   2
HODGE, Samuel   50
HORE-RUTHVEN, Alexander Gore Arkwright   165

KENNA, Paul Aloysius   159

LANE, Thomas   13
LAWSON, Edward   156
LEACH, Edward Pemberton   77

LENON, Edmund Henry 18
LE QUESNE, Ferdinand Simeon 124
LLOYD, Owen Edward Pennefather 133
LUCAS, John 10

MACINTYRE, Donald 61
MACKENZIE, John Henry 172
MACLEAN, Hector Lachlan Stewart 152
MAGNER, Michael 'Barry' 60
MAILLARD, William Job 167
MALCOLMSON, John Grant 6
MANLEY, William George Nicolas 34
MANNERS-SMITH, John 130
MARLING, Percival Scrope 117
MARSHALL, William Thomas 116
McCREA, John Frederick 108
McDOUGALL, John Leishman 17
McGAW, Samuel 66
McKENNA, Edward 24
McNEILL, John Carstairs 33
MELLISS, Charles John 173
MITCHELL, Samuel 36
MOORE, Arthur Thomas 7
MOORE, Hans Garrett 72
MULLANE, Patrick 94
MURRAY, Alexander Edward 150
MURRAY, John 38
MURPHY, Thomas 57

NESBITT, Randolph Cosby 139

ODGERS, William 8
O'HEA, Timothy 49

PENNELL, Henry Singleton 153
PICKARD, Arthur Frederick 29
PITCHER, Henry William 23
PRIDE, Thomas 42

RIDGEWAY, Richard Kirby   101
ROGERS, Robert Montresor   15
RYAN, John   25

SARTORIUS, Euston Henry   85
SARTORIUS, Reginald William   65
SCOTT, Andrew   71
SCOTT, Robert George   102
SEELEY, William Henry Harrison   43
SELLAR, George   93
SHAW, Hugh   39
SMITH, Alfred   120
SMITH, Frederick Augustus   37
SMITH, James   147
SMYTH, Nevill Maskelyne   163
STAGPOOLE, Dudley   27

TEMPLE, William   28
TREVOR, William Spottiswoode   45

VICKERY, Samuel   157
VOUSDEN, William John   92

WATSON, Thomas Colclough   145
WHITCHURCH, Harry Frederick   134
WHITE, George Stuart   83
WILSON, Arthur Knyvet   114
WOOD, John Augustus   4

BIBLIOGRAPHY

Ashcroft, M., *Victoria Cross Heroes* (Headline Review, 2006).

Beckett, I., *The Victorians at War* (Hambledon & London, 2003).

Brazier, K., *The Complete Victoria Cross* (Pen & Sword, 2020).

Crook, M. J., *The Evolution of the Victoria Cross* (Midas Books, in association with Ogilby Trusts, Tunbridge Well, 1975).

Farwell, B., *Queen Victoria's Little Wars* (Allen Lane, Penguin Books, 1973).

Glanfield, J., *Bravest of the Brave: The Story of the Victoria Cross* (Sutton Publishing Ltd., Stroud, 2005).

Haydon, A. L., *The Book of the VC* (Andrew Melrose, 1906).

Holmes, R., *Sahib, The British Soldier in India* (Harper Perennial, 2005).

Ingleton, R., *Kent VCs* (Pen & Sword, 2011).

Knight, I., *Go to Your God Like a Soldier* (Greenhill Books, 1996).

Knight, I., *Marching to the Drums* (Greenhill Books, 2000).

Laband, J., *The Land Wars* (Penguin Books, 2020).

Royal Army Medical Corps, *The Medical Victoria Crosses* (Arrow Press, Aldershot, 1983).

Reid, E., *The Singular Journey of O'Hea's Cross* (Leamcon Press, 2003).

Ross, G., *Scotland's Forgotten Valour* (MacLean Press, 1995).

Smyth VC, Sir J., *Great Stories of the Victoria Cross* (Frederick Muller, 1963).

Smyth VC, Sir J., *The Victoria Cross, 1856-1964* (Frederick Muller, 1965).

The Journal of the Victoria Cross Society, Editions 1-12 (ed. Brian Best, The Victoria Cross Society).

The VC and DSO Book: The Victoria Cross 1856-1920 (ed. The late Sir O'Moore Creagh and Humphris, E.M. (The Naval & Military Press)).

Whitehouse, H., *Battle in Africa* (Field Books, 1987).

Wilkins, P., *The History of the Victoria Cross* (Constable, 1904).

ABOUT THE AUTHOR

Kevin Brazier has long been intrigued by military medals and their recipients, in particular the Victoria Cross (VC), Britain's highest award for gallantry. His study of the VC led to his definitive work *The Complete Victoria Cross,* and he has also written books on the George Cross, the Blue Max and the Knight's Cross. His latest book on the *VCs of Queen Victoria's Little Wars: 1851 - 1901* tells the story of 114 men who were awarded the VC for action during some of the lesser known wars during Victoria's reign.

Also by Barnthorn Publishing:

Henry Hook VC: A Rorke's Drift Hero by Neil Thornton.

Henry Hook is perhaps the most famous private soldier in British military history. It is his portrayal in the movie, _Zulu_, which has cemented this position, but the real Hook was a far cry from the hard-drinking scoundrel that he was portrayed as on screen. Unlike the character in the movie, Hook's record was unblemished, and he received excellent character references from his superiors after leaving the army.

Posted to defend the Rorke's Drift hospital with orders to protect the sick and wounded at the start of the battle, Hook stuck to his task with the utmost determination. Indeed, he was more than willing to lay down his own life in his duty to save the lives of those others who were less able.

Here, Rorke's Drift expert, Neil Thornton, chronicles Hook's life, including his early years, his turbulent marriage, and his later life, putting to bed a number of myths that have developed and grown over the years, whilst analysing Hook's part in the Battle of Rorke's Drift for which he was awarded the coveted Victoria Cross.

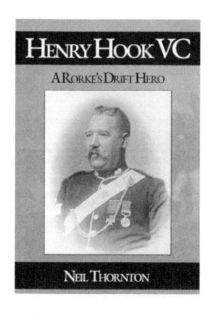